How to Account for Sustainability

A Business Guide to Measuring and Managing

Laura Musikanski

Executive Director and Co-Founder,

The Happiness Initiative

Email: laura.musikanski@gmail.com

First published in 2012 by Dō Sustainability
87 Lonsdale Road, Oxford OX2 7ET, UK

ISBN 978-1-909293-28-1 (eBook-ePub)
ISBN 978-1-909293-29-8 (eBook-PDF)
ISBN 978-1-909293-27-4 (Paperback)

A catalogue record for this title is available from the British Library.

At Dō Sustainability we strive to minimize our environmental impacts and carbon footprint through reducing waste, recycling and offsetting our CO_2 emissions, including those created through publication of this book. For more information on our environmental policy see **www.dosustainability.com**.

Page design and typesetting by Alison Rayner
Cover by Becky Chilcott

For further information on Dō Sustainability, visit our website:
www.dosustainability.com

DōShorts

Dō Sustainability is the publisher of **DōShorts**: short, high-value ebooks that distil sustainability best practice and business insights for busy, results-driven professionals. Each DōShort can be read in 90 minutes.

New and forthcoming DōShorts -- stay up to date

We publish 3 to 5 new DōShorts each month. The best way to keep up to date? Sign up to our short, monthly newsletter. Go to **www. dosustainability.com/newsletter** to sign up to the Dō Newsletter. Some of our latest and forthcoming titles include:

- *Green Jujitsu: Embed Sustainability into Your Organisation* Gareth Kane
- *How to Make your Company a Recognised Sustainability Champion* Brendan May
- *Making the Most of Standards* Adrian Henriques
- *Promoting Sustainable Behaviour: A Practical Guide to What Works* Adam Corner
- *Solar Photovoltaics Business Briefing* David Thorpe
- *Sustainability in the Public Sector* Sonja Powell
- *Sustainability Reporting for SMEs* Elaine Cohen
- *Sustainable Transport Fuels Business Briefing* David Thorpe
- *The Changing Profile of Corporate Climate Change Risk* Mark Trexler & Laura Kosloff
- *The First 100 Days: Plan, Prioritise & Build a Sustainable Organisation* Anne Augustine
- *The Short Guide to SRI* Cary Krosinsky

Subscriptions

In additional to individual sales and rentals, we offer organisational subscriptions to our full collection of published and forthcoming books. To discuss a subscription for your organisation, email **veruschka@dosustainability.com**

Write for us, or suggest a DōShort

Please visit **www.dosustainability.com** for our full publishing programme. If you don't find what you need, write for us! Or Suggest a DōShort on our website. We look forward to hearing from you.

....

Abstract

LEARN HOW TO MEASURE, MANAGE, AND ACCOUNT for sustainability in your business in clear, simple, and feasible steps. This book takes you from concept to innovation and back to action items for all aspects of sustainability. Each chapter has four sections: 1) a specific description of a sustainability challenge, 2) an example of a business making a profit by confronting the challenge, 3) an exercise challenging the reader to identify business solutions and 4) clear, simple takeaways. The book is structured around the world's most accepted guidelines for sustainability reporting, the Global Reporting Initiative (GRI).

About the Author

 **LAURA MUSIKANSKI**, JD, MBA, is Executive Director and Co-Founder of The Happiness Initiative. Prior to joining the Happiness Initiative, Laura served as Executive Director of Sustainable Seattle, and before that she was the Sustainability Director for a medium-sized (US$90m a year) environmental consulting firm and an entrepreneur and small business owner for 18 years. She taught on the University of Washington MBA program as well as for professional training programs. Laura is a lawyer with an MBA and certificates in Environmental Management and Environmental Law and Regulations from the University of Washington. She is a member of the Balaton Group, and has published articles in *YES, Earth Island Institute, CSRWire, Mom's Rising,* and *The Progressive.*

Acknowledgments

Sonja Carson for her championing and belief in this project. Tim Abbe for his long suffering support. Ann Burgund for her creativity and expertise. Ann Prezyna for her friendship and care.

Contents

Abstract..5

About the Author 7

Acknowledgments 9

1   Introduction: Occam's Razor and
    Sustainability Reporting......................15
    So, what is sustainability?................................16
    Areas and aspects of sustainability............17
    How to use this book................................19
    A bit about best practices 19
    How not to use this book 20

2   The Environment: Challenges, Examples,
    and Opportunities 23
    Materials................................23
    Energy................................25
    Transportation................................27
    Emissions, effluents, and waste 29
    Waste................................31
    Water 33
    Biodiversity 35

Products and services 37

Compliance 39

**Overall – environmental protection
expenditures and investments** 41

3 The Economy: Challenges, Examples,
and Opportunities 43

Economic performance 43

Market presence 45

Indirect economic impacts 48

4 Our Society: Challenges, Examples,
and Opportunities 51

Local community 51

Corruption 53

Public policy 55

Anti-competitive behavior 58

Compliance 60

5 Products: Challenges, Examples,
and Opportunities 63

Customer health and safety 63

Product and service labeling 65

Marketing communications 67

Customer privacy 69

Compliance 72

6 Human Rights: Challenges, Examples,
and Opportunities 75
Investment and procurement practices 75
Non-discrimination 78
Freedom of association and collective bargaining ... 79
Child labor 82
Forced and compulsory labor 84
Security practices 86
Indigenous rights 89

7 Labor Practices and Decent Work:
Challenges, Examples, and Opportunities ... 93
Employment 93
Labor–management relations 95
Occupational health and safety 98
Training and education 101
Diversity and equal opportunity 103

8 Conclusion: You Get What You Measure 107
Your company's sustainability assessment 116

References 111

CHAPTER 1

Introduction: Occam's Razor and Sustainability Reporting

THE PRINCIPLE OF OCCAM'S RAZOR states that the simplest explanation is the best as long as it captures all the relevant points. In the words of Einstein, 'If you can't explain it simply, you don't understand it well enough.'

This book explains, in the simplest terms possible, how to account for sustainability. It does this by providing you with an understanding of the landscape of sustainability with entry points for each area and aspect of sustainability. It is written so you can enhance your company's bottom line through the 'triple bottom line'.

If you are reading this book, you probably have an idea that your company is doing a lot when it comes to sustainability, but are not sure exactly how it all fits together. This book gives you an easy entry point into sustainability reporting for your business. It can also be used to create a foundation for your company's sustainability strategy.

This entry point is found indicators. Once you know what to account for, and what your company is already measuring, and so managing, in the sustainability landscape, it is just a series of simple steps to issue your first sustainability report. One of the benefits of creating a sustainability report is you will have a firm understanding of what sustainability means for your business, where you are doing well, and where your gaps are. With this foundation, you will be in a position to take advantage of the opportunities that sustainability presents for your business, form a strategy, and increase profits while helping the planet.

So, what is sustainability?

These days, the simplest way to measure sustainability is the Global Reporting Initiative's framework, known as the 'GRI'. The GRI emerged in reaction to the 1989 *Exxon Valdez* oil spill. A group of socially responsible investors and environmentalists formed the first set of indicators for managing environmental, social, and economic performance. They thought that if business managers had the means to measure the full range of business impacts, disasters like the *Valdez* oil spill could be averted.

The GRI is a set of guidelines created by businesses, governments, advocacy groups, universities, and research organizations. It is a collaborative effort designed to give business managers the measures to manage sustainability. The GRI encompasses six areas: Environment, Economic, Social, Product Responsibility, Human Rights, and Labor Practices & Decent Work (Figure 1).

....

FIGURE 1. The six areas of sustainability

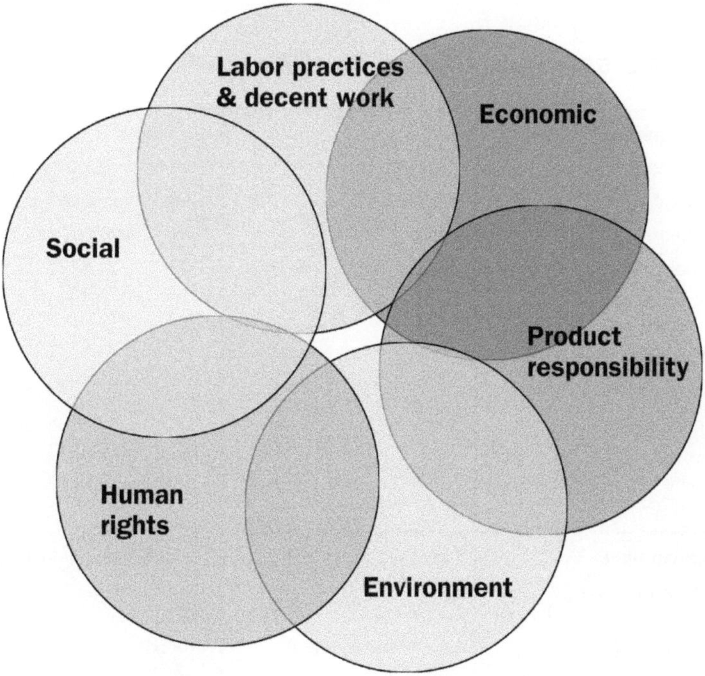

....

The GRI's six areas fit within the convention of the three systems of the 'triple bottom line' – economy, environment, and society. Other areas – labor practices & decent work, human rights, and product responsibility – overlap within environmental, social, and economic systems.

Areas and aspects of sustainability

The 'topography' of the GRI's indicators consists of the areas and the aspects (Figure 2), which can be thought of as the map and the path for business performance, respectively. They are the areas for measuring and for managing.

FIGURE 2. GRI's areas and aspects of sustainability.

Environment	Social	Economic
Materials	Community	Economic performance
Energy	Corruption	Market presence
Water	Public policy	Indirect economic impacts
Biodiversity	Anti-competitive behavior	
Emissions, effluents, & waste	Compliance	
Products & services		
Compliance		
Transport		
Overall – Environmental protection expenditures and investments		
Human rights	**Labor practices and decent work**	**Product responsibility**
Investment & procurement practices	Employment	Customer health & safety
Non-discrimination	Labor–management relations	Product & service labeling
Freedom of association & collective bargaining	Occupational health & safety	Marketing Communications
Child labor	Training & education	Customer privacy
Forced & compulsory labor	Diversity & equal opportunity	Compliance
Security practices		
Indigenous rights		

How to use this book

The following chapters give examples of sustainability challenges and opportunities for businesses within the six areas defined by the GRI. Together, we will look at each specific aspect of sustainability and highlight ways we are not sustainable. For each aspect there is an example of a company that is making good by doing good and an exercise to help business managers identify opportunities within the challenge for enhancing profits and practicing sustainability. At the end of each exercise are learning points the exercise is intended to bring to mind.

A bit about best practices

Best practices are the most efficient and effective way to reach a goal. The businesses I highlight are blazing a new path. Some are doing this intentionally. Others found a niche that emerged out of the lack of sustainability in that industry or market. I use these businesses as examples to inspire. We all understand there are a lot of factors that make for the success, or failure, of a business when it comes to sustainability. Thus, what may work well for one business could end in failure for another. My intent is for the reader to use these examples as launching places to forge their own best practices.

As our environment, society, and economies become sustainable, the best practices for any business will be very different from those of today. Part of our job is creating best practices for doing business that bring about sustainability today and in our future. And then doing it again.

It's that simple, and just like we got what we aimed for at the dawn of the industrial era – profit – we can get what we aim for now by employing simple frameworks, setting simple goals, and creating the best practices that will get us there.

How not to use this book

This book is not prescriptive. It defines sustainability through the GRI, but this does not mean this is the only way to define sustainability for your company. I believe the GRI is a good place to start, but the list of areas and aspects may not cover all the areas where your business is active. The exercises in each area are designed to give you a better perspective on your own business's sustainability performance, and they are also designed to help you identify areas where your business is already working towards sustainability that may not be included in the GRI. In other words, in reading the following chapters think outside the box.

This book is not intended to help you form a sustainability strategy. While strategy is traditionally thought of as necessary before taking action, in some cases, it is not the best first step. A strategy is usually composed of your mission, objectives, tactics, action plans, and resources. You use indicators to manage and measure strategic performance. In this book, I turn this approach on its head. We start with the indicators – the measures. First, you determine what you are already measuring in the sustainability landscape, and then what you can easily measure. From there you have a solid ground to create a strategy.

The purpose of the chapters between this one and the conclusion is to give you the knowledge and framework so you can account for your own sustainability performance. In the conclusion, I ask you to identify all the areas and aspects where you are already measuring performance, and the indicators you are using. By reading the next chapters, you will gain insights and knowledge about your own business's sustainability performance.

CHAPTER 2

The Environment: Challenges, Examples, and Opportunities

IN THIS CHAPTER, YOU WILL FIND PROBLEM STATEMENTS, examples of how a company has profited from the problem, and a short exercise for each aspect of the environment followed by tips. These aspects are materials, energy, water, biodiversity, emissions, effluents & waste, products & services, compliance, transport, and overall environmental protection expenditures and investments.

Materials

What happens when nature's resources, which we rely on, become scarce commodities? The combination of population growth, increased demand for goods by developing nations, and natural resource decline presents a compelling problem, to say the least. Globally, we use over 119 pounds (54 kilograms) of paper products per person a year worldwide.[1] Americans use nearly 661 pounds (300 kilos) of paper per year, where the Nepalese use only about 2.2 pounds (1 kilo) each year. Overall consumption has doubled over the last 40 years. About half of the world's original forests are gone, and within the next 40 years, we could lose the rest.

Bamboo is known as 'poor man's wood'. Over one billion people live in bamboo-framed houses.[2] Bamboo can also be used to produce paper, clothing, and traditional housing materials. Unlike most wood, a bamboo forest can grow in three years. Ann and David Knight saw an opportunity to do the world good and make good in 1994, when they started their bamboo flooring business, Teragren. They kept the company small, wove environmental stewardship into the profit motive, and saw strong growth. They have not yet achieved their goal of being a carbon negative company, but have won recognition for their environmental performance along the way. Today, they have a stronghold in the specialty flooring market, with annual revenues in the double digit millions.

A materials-based strategy

You run an online catalogue firm, selling high-end outdoor gear to retailers and customers. You've converted virtually all your company's paperwork to electronic files, cut back on as much procurement as you could, and adopted a policy you call 'considered decisions' for your procurement and packaging, meaning your managers look at the lifecycle of packaging before contracting with a supplier. Last month you were featured in a national magazine for your forward-thinking packaging. The article was placed next to another covering the law in Germany requiring tech firms to take back their packaging. Now you are getting calls from advocacy groups asking you what you are doing to preserve the forests your customers used to enjoy. What's your plan?

What to think about:

- Connect the dots between your office practices and your product and packaging. Let how you reduce and recycle paper in the office have a ripple effect on your packaging, and for the inputs for your service or product.

- Increase customer retention through recycle, reuse, take back, or renewal programs for your products and packaging.

- Connect your company's well-being to that of the environment: is there a way for your company to use natural and man-made resources that enhances nature or does no harm?

Energy

Most of the world's energy comes from fossil fuels. The United States, where 5% of the world's population resides, consumes 25% of the world's energy.[3] Energy consumption is tied to the gross national product, which is a measure of how much a nation produces per year.[4] If the rest of the world were to require as much energy as the United States, the energy demands would increase by 500%.

Microsoft hired Rob Bernard as their Chief Environmental Strategist when they decided to tackle sustainability. Rob took a three-fold approach, first with the low hanging fruit by reducing energy on their campus. Next, he guided the company to re-engineer their software products for energy efficiency. Last, they developed products for entrepreneurs in the renewable energy market, energy companies seeking to reduce energy use along the supply chain, and data centers seeking higher energy efficiency.

Energetic response

Your online resale company is going gangbusters. It allows the public to freely post items for sale, thereby providing a solution for the 'reuse' part of the mantra 'reduce, reuse, recycle'. You provide a forum for local sales, so that people can zoom into radiuses in five-mile increments when they put in an address, which helps with energy consumption from transportation. Your popularity, and your firm's growth alongside it, has been phenomenal. Last week, potential partners from the EU and from China contacted you. You realize that your business is entirely dependent upon data servers and computers. Your electricity bills tell you that you are using significant amounts of electricity. Your energy provider does too. They are concerned with the drain on their supply to other customers if you are to grow much more. You have tried hard to walk the talk of sustainability, and see your service as important in providing a solution to overconsumption and depletion of natural resources. However now, faced with what seems like the choice of a rock and hard place, you are not sure what to do. What's your strategy?

What to think about:

- Think about closed loop systems or district heating systems. How could the waste in your energy system be used as an input in your system or for another business? Is there a way to redesign a work flow system or could a partnership with a complimentary or other business help reduce energy consumption?

- Do some scenario planning considering a world devoid of the energy supply you are using. How could your business continue to meet its customer's needs?

Transportation

Two-thirds of all oil consumed in America is for transportation. The Energy Information Administration estimates that over 6.5 million barrels of oil are consumed each day in the US. About 95% of transportation in the USA is fueled by petroleum products. The average American consumes 3 gallons per day, while everyone else on the planet consumes an average of just over half a gallon a day. But everyone everywhere is using more gas and the trend keeps going up.[5] Scientists tell us we are now using more oil than the planet's resources can keep up with. In short, if we keep up our levels of consumption, we will use up all of the planet's oil. Most food – from tomatoes to eggs – is carted about 1500 miles before it gets to your plate.[6]

Alice Waters opened her restaurant Chez Panisse in 1972. She saw the need to reconnect people with local and seasonal food. Diners could see the garden where their fruits and vegetables grew, and trace the source of meats and cheeses. Waters's restaurant opened the door for the slow food movement in the United States, and produced a sea-change for restaurants where 'local' can be found on most menus.

Transportation

You started your management consultancy company when you were in grad school, and now it has grown to a national firm with over 100 offices in the USA. Many of your clients are in the energy industry, so you have to be careful how you present your firm. More often than not, your staff drives to client meetings. You have converted all company vehicles to hybrids or biodiesel fuel, use car-sharing programs for offices without cars, and provide full refunds for use of public transportation and incentives for bike use. You are searching to go the next step in terms of your services. What's your plan?

What to think about:
- Adapt your business travel and entertainment policies to encourage video calls and meetings, preferences for energy efficient or hybrid vehicle rental, green or eco-friendly hotels, and restaurants serving organic foods.

- Adopt programs to encourage use of buses and bikes for employee commutes and set policies for distance working and flexible working practices.

> • Include distance and mode of transportation in your calculations when you make purchasing, manufacturing, and supplying decisions.

Emissions, effluents, and waste

For over 2000 years, the levels of carbon dioxide in the atmosphere remained relatively steady at about 280 parts per million. Since the industrial revolution, CO_2 concentration levels have increased by over 30% to about 377 parts per million.[7] While there is much talk of reducing greenhouse gases, the levels continue to increase by about 1.5% per year.[8] The largest contributor to greenhouse gas emissions is electricity production and consumption.[9]

The Intertribal Council on Utility Policy was formed in the mid-1990s to support wind energy projects on native lands in North and South Dakota as well as Nebraska. Nine Native American tribes share the goal of wind energy for all tribal members and a thriving enterprise selling energy to the national and international market. The Council built its first wind turbine project in 2003, partly funded by green energy credits purchased by the US Navy. The Rosebud Sioux tribe receives 750 kW of energy from the project, with plans to increase the power yield. Its second wind energy project powers one tribe's casino, with plans for expansion.

Greenhouse gas powered

Your consultancy/research company just won a big contract with the military to employ a new technology that you spent the last 10 years developing. Now you are finally able to pay some debts and reach solvency with your company. It is a method based on natural systems for converting carbon dioxide into high quality airline fuel. The method is expensive, but dependable and portable, and the output is excellent. You hear about similar projects to yours using sunlight to reformulate carbon dioxide into inputs for the chemical industries. You feel at once elated and saddened. Your mission was to help solve the problem of climate change, and you realize that part of the solution is to reduce carbon dioxide emissions. Your project simply helps to stem growth of GHG emissions. You are just at the beginning of your career, and you realize you could concentrate on gaining more projects like the one you just won, and probably get rich, but you do not feel inspired. Feeling that your work is contributing to a better planet and doing well financially are equally important to you. What's your plan?

What to think about:
- Understand how your business provides solutions to sustainability challenges and clearly communicate the importance of your employees so they feel valued and valuable, and proud of the company.

> • Look beyond your competitors to companies in other industries that are similar to yours in some way. There may be ways to blend technologies to improve your good or service, or opportunities to enter a different or new market or partner with a company in another industry.

Waste

United States residents generate over 250 million tons of waste per year. Waste in the USA increased from 2.68 to 4.62 pounds per person per day between 1960 and 2007.[10] Today, about 100 million tons of garbage floats in a patch of the sea the size of Texas between Los Angeles and Hawaii. Estimates are that it covers from between 0.4% to 8% of the Pacific Ocean. Eighty percent of it comes from land. The other 20% comes from ships. The 'Eastern Garbage Patch' is a mass of disintegrating waste on and below the surface of the sea.[11]

Patagonia joined efforts with Malden Mills to create the first outdoor clothing made from double-faced fleece. Patagonia got its start as a catalogue company selling gear in 1964, and went from zero to two million dollars in four years, climbing to $154 million in 1995. In 1993, Patagonia began making clothing out of recycled soda bottles. In 2005, they set the goal of making all their garments recyclable with its Common Threads program. Customers bring in clothing too worn to be used and the company breaks down the fiber and turns it into new clothing. The company tracks the energy used in recycling the clothing as well as greenhouse gas emissions, miles traveled, and fuel used. They found that recycling clothing emits over 40% fewer greenhouse gases and uses over 70% less energy. Today, while Patagonia runs only a little over 50 stores, they supply over 1000 dealers, in addition to the catalogue and online sales, and they recycle about 48% of their clothing.[12]

Waste not, want not

Last week you received a notice of violation of the Clean Water Act and with the message that you can expect a stiff fine. The notice describes levels of Biological Oxygen Demand (BOD) in the water, which, you know, if it gets high enough, will kill fish and turn the stream into a murky green soup. You know the high BOD levels come from your milk and cheese farm's goat and sheep manure. You advertise that your animals range freely, your products are all natural, and your farm is eco-friendly. You have planted bankside trees and bushes to buffer the river. You know you need to take action. What's your plan?

What to think about:
- Work with local agencies and nonprofits to manage the impact your company has on the environment. If your company has a negative impact on the environment, there is probably a local or national nonprofit that aims to solve that problem. Look for a business-friendly nonprofit or agency that can work with you to

form the plans, gather resources, and implement a solution for your impact.

- Think about your company's waste product as a potential resource for another company. Is there a business opportunity here for you or could you form a partnership with an emerging company to foster a business?

Water

There is physical and political water scarcity. Political water scarcity means there is not sufficient infrastructure to bring clean drinking water to people. Physical water scarcity means there is not enough water. Globally, about 450 million people a year in the world experience water scarcity. By 2025, two-thirds of the world's population will face water scarcity.[13]

One thing the average Indian has in common with the average American is their water consumption – over 1000 gallons of water per day per person.[14] The average steel company in India uses between 10 and 80 cubic meters of water for each ton of steel. In Jamshedpur, India, the wells are running dry. It is also one of the largest industrial areas in India, and home to Tata Steel. The Tata Steel plant installed a closed-loop system for reusing water, new equipment, water, and harvesting systems, as well as cooling ponds designed to capture rainwater. Within 10 years, Tata Steel brought its groundwater extraction to zero, cut water consumption by 67% and reduced pollutants by 98%.[15] Migratory birds populate Tata Steel's cooling ponds and the company is winning awards for its environmental performance.

Water connections

You made your fortune selling water purifiers. Your first line was for the consumer market. These small, sleek, and efficient filters fit easily on the head of a faucet with filters that can be cleaned and re-used. They still have the largest market share of the home water filters market, but the market has been slowly declining over the years. You also sell a popular line of bottled water sourced from the Appalachians that is celebrated for its flavor and have a policy of giving 10% of profits to river, wetland, and shoreline restoration projects. The market has been flooded with water companies, and this line has been barely making a profit in the last three years. Your third line is your newest. It is a small and expensive machine that converts the hydrogen and oxygen in the air into water. Your main consumers for this product are alpine mountaineers and business travelers with hefty expense accounts. Last month, you visited Addis Ababa, Ethiopia, where you met a woman whose child had died from contaminated water, and whose garden crop had turned to dust from lack of water. You are concerned about the future of your business, and have decided that you will include some way to help solve the problems faced by people confronted with water scarcity. What's your plan?

What to think about:

- Look for ways to provide services and goods in markets where there is high need but no or little ability to pay for your product. Is there a way to enter these markets using a different business model, such as community purchasing or reengineering your product to fit the constraints of local?

- Do some scenario planning. Imagine a world where the natural resource your product depends upon, such as water in this example, was scarce for all and the vast majority of customers had very little ability to pay. What would your product or service look like? How would you deliver to market? What would need to happen to stay in business?

Biodiversity

Biodiversity can be defined and measured by the richness and variety of species. The number of threatened animals on our planet went from about 5207 to about 10,615 between 1996 and 2012.[16] The number of threatened plants went from about 5328 to 9165 in the same time span.[17]

Ecotourism restores and conserves nature while earning revenues. Oyster Bay Outfitters and Southeast Expeditions in Virginia take people into the wilderness without damaging the birds, turtles, and marshes, while teaching tourists about species and giving them an experience that will increase their own sense of the value of nature. Both are small businesses and work with the State Department of Environmental Quality to ensure their guides are certified and to promote the idea of protecting biodiversity.

Abundance and scarcity

You began your landscaping business in college as a way to pay tuition for your studies in sociology and history and to spend time in the outdoors. Since then, it has grown to be the largest landscaping business in your state. Eighty percent of your clients are businesses, 15% are residences (most of which are owners or managers of the businesses you serve) and the rest are small government contracts. Of your business activities, 70% are in maintenance and the rest are in design, often working with architects and engineers. Your state's governor just issued an executive order for increased protection of ecosystems in the state, with the first step to be the formation of a steering committee to create a roadmap to effect this goal within the next 50 years. You have already converted most of your products to organics, and substantially reduced use of pesticides, fungicides, and herbicides. Lately, you noticed that your business is slowing, and you suspect that the proliferation of small start-up landscaping companies, many of them single-shingle operations calling themselves restorationists, are eating into your market space. What's your plan?

What to think about:

- Work with the regulatory community to form laws or regulations that level the playing field so all companies in your industry are required to uphold a certain standard. These efforts are often coordinated by a nonprofit and conducted with many different organizations, from businesses to investors, agencies and academics.

- Establish clear criteria for your company's expertise through industry alliances, such as certification programs, or regulations imposed by governments, such as licenses for engineers.

Products and services

In the United States, about 10,000 packaging companies contribute to the production of over 75 million tons of packaging materials per year, which comes to just over 500 pounds of packaging per person.[18] Most of this packaging ends up as garbage in landfills or filling our seas.

Walmart set out to reduce its environmental footprint in the late 1990s. It created a scorecard for their suppliers. Over 150,000 suppliers were expected to reduce item packaging, increase display efficiency, and decrease carbon emissions from transportation. Walmart estimates its program resulted in saving over $10 billion dollars as well as reductions in consumption of about 66 million gallons of fuel and in emissions of 667,000 metric tons of carbon dioxide between the mid-1990s and 2006.[19]

Products and services

Your overnight delivery service is one of the oldest in the country. You have merged and acquired a number of firms and become one of the largest privately run delivery services in the country. However, in the last decade, with the proliferation of electronic transactions, the sales numbers per region are actually declining. You are friends with the General Manager of the Postal Service, and from your conversations with her, the postal service is struggling to survive, and many within the organization question its relevance and the majority of mail delivered ending up in the garbage or recycle bin. Even the holiday burst has waned, replaced with online gift certificates and a push for local procurement in many communities. Like the US Postal Service, you are raising your rates, and you suspect they are soon going to be higher than people are willing to pay. Your have been working on a new business model to save your company from demise. What's your plan?

What to think about:
- Use the creative destruction concept, and think about what it would take to turn a negative impact on the environment into a positive impact. Look to your competitors and emerging new industries that could replace your business and provide solutions to global

sustainability challenges. Is there a way to incorporate what they do into your company that improves your product?

- Think global, act local when business is in decline. Scaling down globally may result, in the end, in a growing business, by tailoring your company to serve smaller scale location-based markets and using or adapting a franchise model.

Compliance

There are three ways to measure compliance with environmental laws and regulations: violations not documented by an agency, violations that receive a notice of violation (NOV), and fines or other sanctions for non-compliance. Environmental fines in the US were $122 million in 2000, and $62.2 million in 2002.[20] Rates of non-compliance for smaller businesses under the Clean Water Act, which protects waterways and watersheds, range from 20% to 75%. On average, smaller businesses violate environmental laws more often than large businesses.[21]

Small dairy farms and dairy processing facilities focusing on compliance in the plant often have a hard time avoiding NOVs.[22] Fresh Breeze Organic Dairy Farm took a different approach. They looked downstream by focusing on water quality and fish habitat protection. They joined with a not-for-profit organization called Salmon Safe that worked with them to plant trees and shrubs to protect the streams and to use a ground cover to keep the soil from eroding into the streams. Their struggle to comply with the environmental laws went away, and they are now one of the leading suppliers to upscale grocery stores of USDA certified organic milk in western Washington.[23]

Compliance

In the early 1990s, when the International Standards Organization issued a set of standards for Environmental Management Systems (EMS), you became director of the EMS division of a large consulting company. At that time, you were director of none. Since then, you grew the department to a staff of 50, with hundreds in the firm working on projects that include EMS work. Most of your clients hired you to help them enter the European market, while some wanted to demonstrate environmental responsibility to their US consumers. Your division enjoyed an extended heyday that ended about three years ago, and since then the firm's management has been treating your division like a cash cow: milking it for the revenue from projects won long ago, and allocating no resources to help maintain or grow the department. In addition, the EPA just passed a law requiring firms over a certain size to have internal EMS departments. While laws sometimes create business opportunities, this one is having the opposite effect. Your prior clients have been hiring your staff left and right, and the growth of in-house work is not helping your department. You are feel you are close to where you were in the early 1990s, and are looking to change that. What's your plan?

What to think about:

- Take the bleeding edge to the cutting edge by defining the market place. In the exercise, the manager has substantial experience in a field that is quickly growing. Teaching seminars (online and in the classroom), offering training, publishing guides, and working with agencies for certification or other schemes can help grow the market and give it stability.

- One of the basic and often overlooked tenets of sustainability is common sense. If where your industry is going follows common sense, what is the next phase in the industry that makes sense, and how can your business move into this space?

Overall – environmental protection expenditures and investments

Brownfields are contaminated sites. This means there are too many toxins in the ground or water for people to safely enjoy the land, or the plants that grow there are too toxic to eat. Sometimes the government declares a site toxic and enforces clean-up, but other times the site is not detected or clean up is voluntary. In the USA there are over 450,000 toxic sites, adding up to about 5 million acres of contaminated land.[24]

P&L Investments buys contaminated sites and flips them. They have bought closed asbestos plants, landfills, and oil refineries. The contamination is cleaned up and the site is turned into a golf course, town homes, parks, or commercial parks. As part of the ventures, P&L Investments partners with other businesses that take a share of the profits.

Green all over, and then some

You are in the last round of a business case competition for which the reward is half a million dollars in seed money to fund the start-up of your idea. Your business plan covered the basis of environmental performance in terms of what it produced and how it is produced. Now you are being asked to come up with five different and separate ideas for green products or services. The criteria for winning are that the ideas be environmentally neutral or beneficial in terms of how they are brought to market and what they are. They must also show innovation and be realistically achievable at not more than the half million dollar range. You have no more than two sentences for each idea. What's your plan?

What to think about:

- See sustainability as synonymous with innovation and continual improvement. There is room for improvement in every decision, every product or service and every activity. Innovation and continual improvement with the aspiration of sustainability and profit are ways to look at business opportunities.

CHAPTER 3

The Economy: Challenges, Examples, and Opportunities

IN THIS CHAPTER, WE EXAMINE THREE ASPECTS of our economy within the GRI: economic performance, market presence, and indirect economic impacts.

Economic performance

When the economy is strong, businesses start up. In the USA, there are about 6 million small businesses employing people and 20 million 'firms without payroll' – meaning one-person businesses. There are only approximately 2000 businesses classified as large businesses – meaning they employ 500 or more people.[25] Most new jobs are created by start-ups.[26] About half a million businesses start up each year.[27] Half of them will make it for more than five years.[28] Unless there is a recession – then fewer businesses start up and more fail.

Alan Greenspan, the former Federal Reserve chairman, blamed the burst of the Dot-Com bubble on 'irrational exuberance'. Between 2000 and 2002, investors in the high tech industry lost $5 trillion dollars.[29] Silicon Valley's unemployment rate went from 3 to 7%.[30] However, half of the high tech businesses survived the bust.[31] Lavish spending and loose control of expenses were features of those businesses that failed.

Regus provides office space and virtual meeting tools so small businesses can reduce costs. The business got its start in 1989 in Europe. Today it operates over 1000 office premises for clients across the globe and generates revenues greater than one billion dollars a year. It struggled through the Dot-Com bust, but regained its profits by focusing on travelers' needs for office space.

Big bang – an ode to economic performance

You got the idea for a parts manufacturing firm that employs and trains the 'unemployable' when you were in high school. In the last 10 years, you have received countless rewards for your business model providing permanent employment for developmentally disabled adults. You just received a product request for twice your facilities' capacity that the buyer needs in short order. The buyer told your marketing director that they chose you because of the social good your business does, and that they intend to heavily market this to their consumers. You're not sure how to meet the demand, and at the same time, have been looking to expand your company's social mission. What are your ideas?

What to think about:

- Mission or purpose statements often fall short of being truly inspiring to employees, management or investors, and customers. A good mission statement inspires and guides a company so that financial health is an outcome, not the aim. Look closely at your mission statement. Can it be expressed in a few words? Does it take your breath away? Does it use simple terms?

- Jobs, rather than profits, are directly linked to economic performance for most people. Reporting workforce alongside profits can be a powerful way to enhance brand. In this example, the company has an opportunity to expand its workforce development and job creation by expanding into new employee pools or partnering with contractors. Often government agencies offer support, including funding for workforce development.

Market presence

People usually think of advertising and other promotional marketing when they think about the market presence of a business. How a business treats its employees and suppliers is also a part of market presence. Wages paid, local hiring, and use of local suppliers can send a powerful message to customers.

It is easy to see the cause and effect relationship between employee treatment and supplier relationships for a small local business. Many small local businesses with a reputation for good treatment of employees, local hiring, and local suppliers have a strong local following. It is harder to see the ties between global businesses and local economies.

Baker McKenzie is a global business that 'thinks locally'. It is one of the largest law firms in the world, currently with 71 offices in 44 countries on every continent with the exception of Antarctica, and brings in over 2 billion dollars a year in revenues. The inspiration for this international law firm comes from the connection between serving the needs of Mexican Americans in Chicago and anticipating the needs of clients trading internationally. Part of its success stems from its practice of staffing offices from the local community and providing partner status to lawyers, regardless of their nationality and location. Another factor is a policy of keeping approximately 75% of revenues among the lawyers in the locations that earned it.

Mind space and market presence

You started a wind sail accessory business seven years ago. Your business has been hovering between small to medium size – fluctuating between 100 and 250 employees, depending on the season and year. Five years ago, you moved operations from Portland, Oregon, to Hood River. You invited your core staff of 75 to come with you and all but five did. The rest of your staff is made up of locals, and for your seasonal employees, you meticulously keep open communication with them and rehire as soon as you can. While you are dedicated to selling through your brick and mortar store, most of your revenues come online or from retail buyers. Last year, you noticed a new trend. Customers are starting to sport tattoos of your logo, and you are seeing more and more of your logo on bumpers and sailboards. You have mixed feelings about this. If you get too hip, and too big, you could fall from grace. On the other hand, your business has been steadily growing in a town that is economically hurting, and you have a passionate following in your staff and your customers. Last month you received 300 applications for jobs. You don't want to miss the train, but don't want to take yourself or your staff on a roller coaster ride. What's your plan?

What to think about:

- In this exercise, the company's brand strength may be at risk through business growth. The formation of subsidiaries allows for growth while protecting the brand. Subsidiaries with their own brands can also explore aspects of a company's sustainability performance and bring those lessons to the main brand. In this case, the company may form a subsidiary that offers complementary products or a similar product for a smaller niche market.

- Seasonality – a product that sells well in one season but is not in demand in another, presents a good opportunity to divest risk. Look to your workforce and office or work floor. What else could you offer with little or no investment? Look at your customers. What do they do in your off-season? How can your brand help you enter that market?

Indirect economic impacts

Indirect economic impacts include infrastructure – such as roads, bridges, ports, public transportation, financial systems, schools, health care, access to water and power, and waste disposal. As Indian business interests found in the 1980s, you need a strong infrastructure for business success.[32] They had attempted to leapfrog the economy with tech companies, but quickly found that businesses could not survive without education, access to clean water and consistent power, and other aspects of infrastructure.[33] Airports were built, schools started, and water utilities formed. Today, India continues to build infrastructure to support business.[34]

The Grameen Bank introduced micro-financing to the world in 1976. Micro-financing is a community-based credit system that uses peer pressure and social relationships to ensure repayment. Loans can be for $1 or a few hundred. The Grameen Bank has provided over 6.55 billion US dollars in loans with a recovery rate of over 95%. Since their inception, they spurred the formation of other micro-credit businesses and nonprofits. In 2006, it was the first business to receive a Nobel Peace Prize.

> ## Making good, doing good, making a difference: Indirect economic impacts
>
> You were a rebel as a kid, and caused your parents more than a few sleepless nights. Luckily, your uncle took you under his wing at an early age. You became the go-to guy for any demolition needed for his commercial construction business. You earned enough

money over one summer of working to buy your first piece of demo equipment, and went into business doing small jobs for him and others in his field. Over the last 20 years, your demolition business has slowly grown so that now you have six core employees and 10 more you hire on an as-needed basis. Lately, you have needed them less and less. Over the years, you have also matured, and have two children of your own. Last week your daughter, just entering 7th grade, came to you with a report she did on a home entirely made out of recycled materials. Your competitor just announced they are committing to cutting in half the waste they send to landfills. You have noticed your sites are getting more visits from regulators interested in storm water runoff. You just won a new job that will allow you enough profit to reinvest some into your business. While you are not going to give up your old markets and services, you are thinking about adding a new direction to your business. Today, you are thinking of five potential new directions. What are they?

What to think about:

- Zero waste is the idea that nothing goes to the waste stream, and everything is reused. Sometimes small steps are better than big ideas, and sometimes it's better to take those small steps with help from others. Look for partnerships with another company that benefits by bearing your burden and increases your efficiency.

- A zero-waste world requires deep systematic change. In this example, the company does not have the power to recycle or reuse everything. Working with a nonprofit that works with organizations within a system – in this case building material manufactures, architects and designers, builders, demolishers, and waste managers – to discuss the notion and issues of zero waste can be a good step towards better business and a better planet and help a business to gain an edge in the marketplace.

CHAPTER 4

Our Society: Challenges, Examples, and Opportunities

IN THIS CHAPTER, WE COVER FIVE ASPECTS of society in the GRI: community, corruption, public policy, anti-competitive behavior, and compliance.

Local community

A community assessment is usually the first step in measuring and managing a company's impact on the local community. In these assessments, a company works with the community to determine the areas of impact. Common issues are gender equity, toxins, and homelessness. About 1.6 million people use a homeless shelter each year, and many are turned away due to lack of beds.[35] Approximately 744,000 people are homeless in a given year.

At first glance, FareStart is a restaurant and coffee bar. At a closer look, it is a nonprofit that operates more like a business. Homeless people are educated and trained as cooks, baristas, waiters, and restaurant managers. It got its start in 1988, and earned about $750,000 in 2008. Popular restaurants in the Seattle area including Dahlia Lounge, McCormick & Schmick's, have hired FareStart graduates.

Creating community

Since you were a child, you had a flair for throwing a party and were a quick read of personalities. You majored in communications and public affairs in college, and after working a few years for big business, started your own event-planning company. You are well networked in the Hispanic and Asian communities, and many of your events incorporate traditional foods, ceremonies, décor, and entertainment. You have a reputation for bringing in the new while respecting tradition. Most of your business has come from the celebration and commemoration event-planning markets, but lately you have done a few promotional events. You distinguish your events from those of your competitors by subtly including traditional Hispanic or Asian flavors. These have been popular in the Hispanic and Asian business community, but some of your long-term clients are disgruntled. Last week you had two cancellations from old clients. In addition, you are being asked by a nonprofit to provide the carbon footprint for each event you hosted last year. You believe that problems represent opportunities, and are determined to surmount these challenges. What is your plan?

What to think about:
- Community and culture are interlinked, and where there is a strong sense of community there is often a strong demand for goods and services that represent that culture. Clearly understand your markets and how

you can protect the strength of one market's culture while operating in the general marketplace. This can be as simple as a statement on your product or service offering materials that explain the importance of your product to that culture and hence educate the general market so it values and preserves a community and culture by purchasing your goods or services.

- Once you have a clear idea of your market, map them to sustainability and look for connections. Take actions towards sustainability that are valued by your customers. In this case, the business's customers may not care too much about a greenhouse gas inventory, but may care a great deal about local suppliers and traditional ways. Focusing on these objectives may decrease energy use and hence greenhouse gases.

Corruption

Corruption is defined as acting dishonestly, unlawfully, or immorally. Corruption eventually leads to disastrous results. The Transparency International Corruption Perceptions Index ranks a country's corruption on a scale of 1 to 10.[36] In 2011 New Zealand was deemed the least corrupt at 9.5 and Somalia and Myanmar the most (1 and 1.5 respectively). The USA ranked 7.1, in 24th place, out of the 182 countries surveyed. Between 2008 and 2011, the United States Justice Department collected over

$3.6 billion in fines from companies ranging from Siemens to Johnson & Johnson for bribes.[37]

Ben & Jerry's ice cream is the poster-child business in the sustainability field. Its success may be due to its values: environmental sustainability and social and economic justice. It started in 1978 with $12,000, sold $4 million of ice cream in 1983, and $148 million in 1994. By the time it was scooped up by Unilever for 326 million, it was earning half a billion a year.[38] Six years after the acquisition, the founders re-joined the company to lead a program on the government's allocation of funds from bombs to children's programs.[39]

Clear communication lines: Corruption

You began work as a private investigator working for one of the larger PI firms straight out of college as a sociology and criminal justice dual major. Since then, you have risen to head the Eastern European Region of your firm. Most of your business is pre-employment and legal compliance screening for US firms looking to expand into Eastern Europe. Your last three clients have made your company a good profit. However, you wonder how much of your work stems from poor understanding of legal standards and laws, and whether your workload would have been lighter if the companies investing in Eastern Europe had known more about the regulatory climate. You noticed that a law firm that works with your clients is offering seminars on the regulatory schemes in Eastern European countries. This could take business away from you. You have an idea for a twist on the compliance services you already offer. You are just about to meet your boss, and are preparing the pitch.

What to think about:

- Efficiency and idealism: envision the way your business would operate in a perfect world. Is there a business today closing the gap between today's reality and that perfect world? What can you offer that pushes your business ahead of others but still allows you to keep hold of your market? Is there a way to streamline your process and solve your customers' problems? In this example, a complementary business is competing through educational services. The business may offer informational brochures and other materials as a way of demonstrating expertise, providing value, and bringing in business. They may also reach out to the competitor to join them in the seminars or offer webinars and video recorded talks to directly compete by educating the market.

Public policy

Since 2008 over $3.5 billion a year has been spent by businesses lobbying the federal government.[40] In 2008, the auto industry spent about $50 million lobbying Congress for loans to the auto industry that amounted to $25 billion.[41] Over $140 million was spent by the finance industry to secure a $700 billion bailout.[42,43] Many businesses that received bailout money continue to lobby Congress.[44]

The State of Illinois Corporate Accountability program tracks tax credit programs.[45] Between 2004 and 2007, Wm Wrigley Jr's Company received about $150,000 dollars in tax credits to fund training programs. Over the course of the credits, 200 jobs were created or saved due to the training program. In 2008, the family-run business, which had seen four generations of Wrigleys at the helm, was acquired by Mars.

Front page test: Public policy

Your public relations (PR) company specializes in helping medium-sized businesses with difficult issues. Your tactic is to help your client identify and implement new projects that remedy a wrong. You base all you do on the 'front page test': never do anything you would not want to see reported on the front page of a newspaper. You have done well with this approach, and have a staff of over 100 across the country, with revenues close to $25 million and a nice profit margin. You just signed on five new clients with deep pocketbooks. Three are headquartered in the United States, one in Japan, and one in Australia. For all, their problems revolve around bailout funds received by the government and bonuses paid to top managers. You perceive a need for PR help in managing issues that arise from going after or receiving public money. You are thinking of a new approach to this issue and are looking forward to opening up this part of the market.

What to think about:

- Directly address a difficult issue. Companies that find themselves in hot water can wait for the issue to blow over, counter or divert, or take direct action. A good first step is to closely examine the message behind an attack on a company for a gap in your company's ethics. From here, a company can set policy, programs, and goals to remedy that gap. Tie this activity to sustainability.

- Sometimes sustainability can get a company in hot water. A company claiming to do right found to be practicing contrary to its policies can get bad press and even sued. In this case, denial can put the company into deeper trouble. Understand your role within a flawed system and the need for all players to work together. Communicating this can be an effective strategy. For example, a clothing company with a fair labor policy found using offshore suppliers employing children could work with other companies using similar suppliers, local governments, international unions and labor organizations, and supplier middle men to solve a problem that many companies share.

Anti-competitive behavior

Anti-competitive behavior was outlawed by the Sherman Anti-Trust Act of 1890 and other acts that followed. Examples of anti-competitive behavior include price-fixing where two or more companies agree to charge the same price, dividing territory where companies agree not to compete in each other's territories, and dumping when the price on something is set so low the competition goes out of business, and then the price is brought back up. In 2012, the European General Court upheld a decision to fine Microsoft over $1 billion for a type of exclusive dealing when the company required retailers to pay a royalty on any computer sold, even if it did not carry Microsoft operating software.

Linux is a free operating system that spurred the creation and expansion of soft and hardware businesses supplying governments, educational facilities, and businesses. It was started as a volunteer project in 1991. It was licensed, rather than copyrighted, under a system that ensured the code was free to use. Today, businesses including Dell, IBM, and Nokia make a profit by offering installation, support, and hardware for Linux operating systems.

Playing fair: Anti-competitive behavior

You started your music label in the grunge era and rode the wave to the top. You stayed on top because you stick to your core-value drivers – delivering public relations and cutting-edge marketing for your musicians and high quality product to the public. Your business has done well compared to some of your competitors, many of whom are much larger than you. You are surviving the onslaught of programs that allowed for free, albeit illegal, loading of music and the explosion of i-Tunes. You have done this by sticking to your core values. Lately something has you worried: the proliferation of self-published and free downloads on Facebook, YouTube, and other free online sources are creating a whole new competitive environment for the music industry. You are seeking a way to continue to deliver cutting-edge marketing to your musicians, and draw new talent to you and customers to your label by creating the market space instead of chasing it. What is your plan?

What to think about:

- Downsize and reorganize: sometimes when an industry is in decline, the only option is to downsize and reorganize. Downsizing opens doors to hyper-local or niche market specialization. When downsizing, look for ways to creatively use the technologies that are replacing you to support the emerging structure of your business. While this can be a painful process, and often involves letting go of ways of doing business that brought both great success as well as layoffs, and profit loss, it can lead to new and innovative business forms.

- Resize: if your industry is dying, you may be able to reinvent your business for a niche market that caters to a hyper-local market. There may be other areas with similar market conditions that would welcome your smaller business.

Compliance

Between 2009 and 2011, 222 criminal cases were brought against companies for anti-trust violations.[46] Over $2 billion in fines were imposed. Over 45,000 people have been incarcerated. But the costs of non-compliance go beyond fines and imprisonment. Companies take a hit to their reputation. Often the legal costs and staff time are as costly as the fines. And when there are large scandals, the damage is felt by many. Arthur Anderson, formerly one of the 'Big Five' accounting firms, paid the ultimate price in non-compliance when it did not fulfill its promise to ensure that its clients were compliant with accounting rules. The company closed its doors in 2002 and 85,000 people lost their jobs.

In the mid 1990's both Gap and Nike adopted codes of conduct that required factories to be in compliance with local labor laws.[47] Nike reported full compliance in labor practices when, in fact, corporal punishment, sexual abuse and child labor were not uncommon. Nike's denial of working conditions got them in hot water – an eight-part expose in the New York Times and a lawsuit followed their denial. Gap took a lesson from Nike, and decided to practice transparency. Their reports give details by country and factory of their struggles to bring factories into compliance and accounts of factories out of compliance with local laws, child labor prohibitions, forced labor and other unfair labor practices. Gap's approach has been to work in partnership with non-profits, unions, governmental agencies and other organizations to bring factories into compliance. They also opened avenues of communication along the supply chain so inventory managers understand the pressure of rush orders or poorly timed orders on factory managers, and the actors along the supply chain could work together to ensure fair labor and timely inventory supply.

Competing through compliance

You started your environmental health and safety-consulting firm 30 years ago and have successfully taken a large part of the market share of companies dealing with contamination issues. Today, you have over 100 offices with 2300 staff. You want to enter the climate change market, and have formed some new services. You hired a sustainability and climate change practice leader who leads a team of 10, but even within your firm, your staff is having a hard time making the connection between contamination and climate change. Every year, your firm donates staff and time to a volunteer project in a developing nation. Last year your firm's volunteer project worked with volunteer organizations in cleaning up a contaminated site in Mexico. The project included carbon sequestration and mediation of the transfer of the credits. You are watching smaller boutique firms take this market from you with increasing projects awarded out from under you. You are eager to take this market segment, as is your sustainability and climate change team, and are looking for other ways to help the team.

What to think about:

- Think international: in the US the sustainability market is mostly voluntary. Look to a country where there are laws leveling the playing field. How do those companies operate? What do their revenues and profits look like? What can you translate to your company? If the market in the US is too small or demand too low, is there a way to serve companies in those countries seeking to enter your market?

- Steer your company's volunteer projects towards emerging products and markets. If your company donates staff time to a volunteer project each year, choose a big challenge that could foster client development and a new business line, as well as develop staff. Companies that use this approach often have their marketing showcase the project. Make sure your marketing team is making the links between the new market or service, new clients and staff development.

CHAPTER 5

Products: Challenges, Examples, and Opportunities

IN THIS CHAPTER, WE COVER FIVE ASPECTS of product responsibility within the GRI: customer health and safety, product and service labeling, marketing communications, customer privacy, and compliance.

Customer health and safety

In 2007 there were massive recalls for toys that contained lead in the United States, India, and other countries.[48] Mattel was fined over $14 million by the US Consumer Product Safety Commission and ended up paying about $2.3 million. Mattel shareholders filed a resolution against the company for failing to disclose information in a timely manner. Parents filed a class action lawsuit for a fund to monitor their children for lead poisoning.[49]

Green Toys is a company that offers non-toxic toys made from recycled and recyclable materials. The company got its start in 2007 with four toys. Within two years, it more than doubled its line, and quickly grew from a supplier to a few small boutiques to supplying global chains including Pottery Barn Kids and FAO Schwartz.

The precautionary principle: Customer health and safety

Your cleaning product company has provided products to hospitals and other health care organizations for 300 years. In the last five years, you entered the consumer market and are gaining market share. Most people associate your brand with good health, and for good reason. Your forefather started the business in Europe when the link between disease and unsanitary surroundings became clear. But last month you got some bad press. A national news show highlighted your company's products as potential endocrine disruptors and linked your products to human health issues and fish kills. Every day you are receiving letters from concerned customers and your health care clients are asking questions. You launched a green-sideline of your cleaners last year, and it is slowly growing. You are laying a plan to address your customer's concerns, protect your company's reputation, and ensure a secure business for the future.

What to think about:

- Health and safety threats can quickly stall a market or product. When a company cannot readily replace an ingredient or input, it can lose its market share. When a disaster hits, companies will scramble and compete to find replacements. Companies can join or form coalitions of similar companies to stay abreast of health and safety threats and ensure adequate suppliers of safe materials for a market.

- Keep ahead of the curve with different strategies. A blog on your company website can be a good way to get an early warning of customer health and safety concerns. Look for a nonprofit or agency that researches and educates the public about toxins in your industry. Get familiar with the standards of a country with a higher bar for health and safety protection laws, such as many Northern European countries.

Product and service labeling

It was not until 1990 that nutritional labeling was required. Before that, labeling laws required honest and informative labels, but they did not state what needed to be labeled. Cocaine first entered the market as an addition to alcohol for cocktails. With Prohibition came the invention of a soft drink, Coca-Cola (coca for cocaine). In 1903, the addictive qualities of cocaine became apparent and since then Coca-Cola has instead used the coca leaves from which cocaine is removed.

Timberland Co. is a shoe company that includes greenhouse gas emissions, chemical composition, hours of labor, and country of origin information on its labels. They worked in partnership with nonprofits to create a Green Index tool. The effort to label their products with sustainability factors also led to streamlined data collection and improved communication between the factories and headquarters.

Talking the walk: Product and service labeling

Your natural foods company just celebrated 20 years of business. You are the cornerstone of the natural food snack market. You realize you have opened the door for many entrepreneurs. Sharing information is an important value to your company. Your products have always carried extensive labeling, including labels for organic, trans-fats-free, non-GMO, growth hormones-free. You want to take your labels to the next level, and include information about fair trade ingredients, your use of renewable energy, and other socially responsible and eco-friendly practices. However, you are concerned about clutter, and while buyers may find your message interesting, you suspect that purchasing decisions are based on health concerns. Still, you are determined to find a way to communicate what you are doing, if only to set an example for the many others in the natural food market. What's your plan?

What to think about:

- Communicate on multiple levels: your project may have a few eco-labels or other information about sustainability. You can add a short sustainability report card with your label, including three or four indicators. On your company website you may have one page or a poster that explains more, and then a more detailed report. Use multiple kinds of social media to point people to this information.

- Communicate relevance: it's not enough to say you are reducing greenhouse gas emissions or using just so many units of energy for a product. Customers need to understand how this makes your company better than others and how it impacts their lives and the lives of their children. Connect the dots and tell this story in your communications materials.

Marketing communications

Marketing has two purposes: information and persuasion. In the late 1970s, Nestle marketed baby formula to West African nations using a campaign aimed at persuading breast-feeding mothers to switch to formulas. Instructions about mixing the formula, warnings about use of contaminated water, or information about the benefits of mother's milk were not understandable to the illiterate and sometimes missing from the product. Because Nestle was entering a market of mostly poor people, the mothers would cut down the amount of formula, leading to malnourishment in their children. Boycotts in the United States, Canada, Europe, Australia, and New Zealand ensued. International organizations joined to form an International Code of Marketing of Breast-milk Substitutes. Nestle agreed to follow the code and the boycotts were officially called off.

Puget Sound Consumer Cooperative Grocery Chain (PCC), the largest cooperative grocery in the USA, launched a marketing campaign to children focused on expanding palates for healthy food. Food marketing to children is about a $10 million a year industry in the United States.[50] PCC's marketing is hands-on. With the 'kids picks' program, children are offered samples of a food and asked to rate it. Foods are sold at the store and range from frozen fruit to spaghetti sauce. Foods that kids like are labeled as a 'kids pick' in the store.

Marketing communications

You started a small newspaper catering to the X-generation in the late 1980s in Pittsburgh, Pennsylvania. The paper was a success, and since then you have newspapers in over 100 cities in the USA. All of your papers are published in print and online. Seven years ago you started a local television station in Austin, Texas that was a success. You now have 15 stations across the nation and continue growing this end of your business. You have always thought of yourself as an environmentalist, and started an online journal, Eco-Expressions, reporting science-based information about climate change, renewable energies and biodiversity through podcasts and other interactive formats four years ago. This journal has yet to make a profit, and last year, your company's overall performance was not stellar. You did not show a loss, but it was close. You own a majority share in your companies, but you are getting some pressure to close the journal. Meanwhile, last quarter, a small constituency of shareholders filed a resolution demanding that all your media focus more on climate change and renewable energies. You are dedicated to Eco-Expressions, and have tinkered with the idea of changing it into a nonprofit, but are not particularly taken with this idea. In any case, the entrepreneurial spirit is stirred, and you are looking for a way to perk up profits and answer the seemingly conflicting demands of your shareholders. Your ideas?

What to think about:
- Integration: often companies enter the sustainability market place with new products or services. Once these have become established, and if the market is not growing or bearing the product, it may be time to merge sustainability into your main line and brand.

- Different business formations: social entrepreneurs and for-benefit corporations are emerging forms of business that operate like businesses in the marketplace but are not-for-profits behind the scenes. Your sustainability business line may benefit from spinning off into one of these new forms of business.

Customer privacy

Private information includes age, gender, telephone number, social security number, sexual orientation, and cultural or social identity. In many industries, protection of personal data is guided by an honor system.[51] In 1995, the European Commission issued directive 95/46/EC. This law restricts gathering and use of personal information. In 2002, the US Congress passed the Sarbanes Oxley Act, nicknamed 'SOX'. SOX requires companies to have anonymous whistleblower programs such as ethics hotlines. McDonald's instituted a whistleblower hotline in Europe that allowed employees to report management misconduct. The French government attacked it because there was no process for ensuring the integrity of the information reported. This was because callers were anonymous. Eventually, compromises were made, and anonymous hotlines became confidential, access to the reported information was restricted, and the personal data was quickly deleted once acted upon.

Trust-e operates as a consulting organization offering privacy policies and programs, certifications, stakeholder management, and mediation to online businesses. Trust-e also verifies compliance with the International Safe Harbor Privacy Principles. Trust-e began business in 1997, and serves over 3000 web-based businesses, including eBay, Facebook and Linked-in.

Creating community: Customer privacy

You have been running small coffee shops in Atlanta since the 1970s. Your shops continue to be successful, and you have amassed a small fortune from them over the years. You see the key to your success as continually demonstrating that your cafes are part of, and even help maintain, the community. One way you create community is by covering your walls with cork and allowing anyone to post what they like as long as it is relevant to the neighborhood. When customers go online, they are directed to your homepage, which is an electronic billboard for each location that anyone can post to. Sometimes the degree of personal information people share on the page surprises you. Four years ago, you started tracking your cafés' greenhouse gas emissions. You include electricity use, refrigerants, your suppliers' and employees' commutes. You see this as another way to demonstrate how your business supports the community. One of your newer employees just sent you a complaint that the questions posed to her about her commutes were a violation of her privacy. You feel that it is important to address her concerns and want to make sure your customers who post to your billboards, both virtual and not, enhance the community without putting anyone's privacy in danger. Also, you would also like to find a way to recoup some of your costs for the internet service, but fully intend to keep it free for customers. Your ideas?

What to think about:

- Use common sense: often when a company is 'doing good' and operating in the sustainability field, they can get carried away with the technical elements or idealism. It's important to ground sustainability and community efforts in common sense. Clearly communicate what you are doing and why in simple terms.

- Use clear codes: you can ground your personal data privacy code in the European Union's Protection of Personal Data Directive 95/46/EU, the code that offers the greatest protection, but make sure you translate this into simple and understandable terms. In the example, a clear and unmistakable message that personal information is voluntary and how it would be used could have avoided the problem in this case.

Compliance

Manufacturers and marketing in the USA have been regulated by government since the 1600s.[52] The public also has a role in regulating. This is called 'license to operate'. The Occupy Movement, begun in 2011, is an example of the public impact on the license to operate. In spring of 2012, the Occupy Movement focused on the Bank of America with protests across the country.[53] The press picked this up, and a number of customers switched banks.

Apollinaris and Dasani are two bottled waters sold by The Coca-Cola Company. In 2004, they set a target of 100% compliance with waste water laws at bottling facilities and designated compliance levels in countries where laws or infrastructure were lacking. In 2006, the company reported over 80% compliance, and by 2011, 96%. The compliance program set the groundwork for water use reduction in their plants, water source protection for its plants across the globe, and programs to address water scarcity in Africa.

Compliance: It's all in the water

VitaSoda company uses 80 million liters of water per year to produce 33 million liters of soda. Its strongest markets are in China and areas of the Middle East, but the company's headquarters is in New Delhi, India, where over 170 million people do not have access to safe drinking water. Over the last five years, you have managed to bring all of your facilities – in India and other countries – to compliance levels required by the Indian government. Yesterday your daughter showed you a hate website aimed at all soda companies blaming them for infant mortality and low life expectancy due to water scarcity in India and neighboring countries. A little digging showed the website is being run by a small group of students. Your PR department got a call from Greenpeace yesterday. Your company was mentioned. Your daughter asked you what you are going to do.

What to think about:
- When possible, work with your adversaries to find solutions. In this case, a solution is likely a combination of technology, greater efficiency, and community involvement. If your adversaries are students or youth, you may work with a university or community college to present a prize challenge to teams to solve a problem with set constraints. If your adversaries are not willing to work with you, find a similar group with a different orientation toward business to work with.

CHAPTER 6

Human Rights: Challenges, Examples, and Opportunities

IN THIS CHAPTER, WE COVER FIVE ASPECTS of human rights within the GRI: investment and procurement practices, non-discrimination, freedom of association and collective bargaining, child labor, forced and compulsory labor, security practices, and indigenous rights.

Investment and procurement practices

Conflict diamonds are diamonds that come from war zones where there is no rule of law. Diamond conflicts have led to approximately 3.7 million deaths in Angola, Liberia, Sierra Leone, and the Democratic Republic of Congo.[54] Other human rights abuses from diamond conflicts include forced labor, dangerous working conditions, and cruel treatment of workers and their families.

The Kimberly Process Certification Scheme was introduced by the United Nations to trace the origins of diamonds and end the market for blood diamonds. Ben Bridge Jewelry, a subsidiary of Warren Buffet's Berkshire Hathaway Inc., participates in the program. Ben Bridge Jewelry works with miners and other jewelers at the source to help install processes that strengthen human rights and environmental protection. As members of the Council for Responsible Jewelry Practices, they also work to ensure miners' health and safety. On-site diamond cutting training programs graduate students who are encouraged to start their own businesses cutting diamonds.

The supply chain: Investment and procurement practices

Your parts manufacturing firm has averaged about $90 million a year in revenues for the last five years. When you opened your business, you set a policy preferring local suppliers. At that time, less than 20% of your suppliers were local. Today, more than 80% are local. You are not sure but suspect your policy has contributed to the success and growth of other businesses. Your buyers are asking you to help them comply with their chief buyers' packaging requirements, for which there are nine components that must be reported:

- Greenhouse gases/carbon dioxide per ton of production
- Material value – how much raw material is used to create the package
- Product/package ratio – how small a package is used for the product
- Cube utilization – ratio of packaging to the product
- Transportation impacts – miles traveled, energy use, and emissions
- Recycled content in the package
- Recovery value of the packaging material (e.g. calories for incineration)

- Renewable energy used to produce the package

- Packaging innovation.

You have been working on a way to comply with the request from your buyers and do so in a way that enhances the competitive advantage of your business and that of your buyers. Your ideas?

What to think about:
- Optimization and economies of scale: look for ways to optimize results for one goal by achieving another goal. In this case, increasing cube utilization should decrease transportation and hence greenhouse gases. Look for ways to use economies of scale in your sustainability efforts. In the example, applying the requirements to all products could result in overall cost savings. Lay out the ways to optimize results before taking action, and then look for economies of scale.

- Go lean or reduce and refuse: is there a way to get rid of a step, packaging, or material input without decreasing the value of your project or service? Sometimes the highest impact we have towards sustainability is in not doing something.

Non-discrimination

Discrimination takes the form of lower pay, lack of opportunities, or fewer benefits. Some of the harms of discrimination include children who grow up not believing they have potential, adults who can't find work, and communities that fall apart. Between 1994 and 2004, sexual harassment claims rose by 29%, sexual discrimination claims rose 12%, and age discrimination claims filed by women rose by 39%.[55] In 1979, women earned 62.5% of men's wages. In 1993, women earned 77.1% of men's wages and in 2009, 80% of men's wages.[56]

Wesleyan College opened in 1839 with the aim of educating women in an age when all other universities and colleges catered to men. It was the first college for women in the United States, and now there are over 60 colleges for women in the USA and many more globally.

Non-discrimination

Last year your firm grossed over $10 million in sales. You entered the baby diaper industry with a new eco-friendly product that is price competitive with other disposables and much better for the environment. You know you are about to lose your early entry position, and that you need to re-think how you address the market place. While at a conference where you received an award, you heard a panel discussing research findings indicating that increasing women's education by 1 percentage point leads to an increase of annual GDP growth rates by 2%. (Findings by Sandra Lawson from Global Economic Paper No: 164, Goldman Sacks, March 2008.) The panel sparked some ideas for you. What's your plan?

What to think about:

- Social marketing: how can you tie your product to information that grows your market, protects the well-being of your customers, and increases customer loyalty? You can embed a societal issue into your marketing campaign overtly or by inference. You can also ally your company with a social cause by supporting organizations that work for causes. Co-branding on your products or on the organization helps to foster the alliance in customers' minds.

- Look closely at your workforce and board: are they concerned about discrimination? Do they share the company's social cause, if there is one? Do they represent a diverse workforce or have experience working with diverse populations? If not, it might be best to start internally with education and training about an issue. Include a way for employees and a path for board members to give their ideas for the company.

Freedom of association and collective bargaining

Collective bargaining is a group effort by employees to negotiate work conditions with employers. Freedom of association is the right for any worker to join other workers in a group effort. Both are basic human rights under the United Nations Universal Declaration of Human Rights. The number of union members in the United States reached a peak in the 1950s at 15 million. By 2011, membership rates slowed and there were only 14.7 million union members.[57] The decline in membership is blamed in part on the economy's transition from production of goods to services and also in part on more and more companies taking an anti-union stance.

Choice of entity is another approach to worker rights. Green Workers Cooperative fosters the creation of cooperatives in South Bronx, New York. Rebuilders Source is one of their members. Rebuilders Source resells materials recovered from structures that are being renovated or demolished. The two organizations help each other in marketing and by educating customers about the value to the community, environment, and local economy of purchasing from Rebuilders Source.

Choice of entity: Freedom of association and collective bargaining

You and your partner began your IT business as a partnership. Demand for your services quickly grew, and you and your partner brought in friends and family to help meet demand. At 15 employees, you reincorporated as an Employee Stock Ownership Plan (ESOP). The employee-owners elected a board of directors. New rules were set up so that a new employee had to work one continuous year before gaining the option of ownership. Since then, the company has grown to over 1000 staff. Ten years ago, the board, at your advice, raised the tenure requirement for the

---

right of ownership to three years. You and your partner have been hearing rumors that you are losing junior staff to your competitors because of feelings of inequity. At the same time, Wall Street is condemning your business as inefficient. You and your partner have been planning to make a presentation to the board to address the issues of retention and efficiency. What's your plan?

What to think about:

- Unions provide a way for employees to have a voice in decisions that affect their jobs. In some European countries, unions have been replaced by workers councils. A company can mimic this approach by forming worker groups so employees have a forum and means to voice concerns and communicate with management.

- Equity and comparisons to others: if employees feel they are unfairly compensated, they are more likely to experience job dissatisfaction. Clear guidelines and expectations for profit-sharing, company ownership, and other compensation can assuage feelings of unfairness.

- Choice of entity is an important decision, as it is difficult to change once a business is up and running. If a business has grown to a stage that it is better off in a different entity formation, it is important to

> understand the choices and the benefits and risks for
> each entity.

Child labor

The International Labor Organization (ILO) began an international programme on the elimination of child labor in 1992. The ILO estimates there were 218 million children working worldwide in 2004, with over half in the worst forms of child labor – slavery, armed forces, prostitution, and drug trafficking. The rest work in industry and agriculture.[58]

Senda Athletics distinguishes its soccer equipment on the basis that it is free of child labor and unfair working conditions along the entire supply chain. The company provides soccer balls and equipment to nonprofits working with children. Senda also uses many channels of social media to get the message out about fair trade, youth development, and social entrepreneurship. The business began in 2010, and has increased its offerings to other sport balls as well as apparel.

Child labor

Your firm has been selling chocolate bars to schools for fundraisers for over 100 years. Your company has won multiple awards and mention for its good treatment of workers and its environmental practices. Last month you read an article in an airline magazine linking child trafficking and chocolate farms. The article stated

---

that a study by UNICEF indicated that up to 200,000 boys under 14 are working in slavery condition on farms in the Ivory Coast. You are aware that the Ivory Coast is by far the largest supplier of cocoa beans, but do not know if your company ultimately sources its beans from there. Your competition does not include what you think of as designer chocolates, but you are aware that many of these companies are now sporting a fair labor label. You do not think there is much risk your buyers will ask you about your source of cocoa beans, but if they did, you do not have an answer. You realize you need to have one. What's your plan?

What to think about:
- Understand the risks of inaction: if you are operating in a market where the niche is catering to a grave or ethically charged concern, ensure you are fully aware of the impacts of your business. In the example, if the business is supplied by child labor, it is important to know the impact on your customers to gauge the urgency of the issue. It is also important to know the outcomes for the children if you switch suppliers. Might they end up in worse working conditions? If so, it may be better to approach the situation by joining forces with other businesses and through an agency.

- Work with suppliers, and customers: if you find your business is dependent upon a supplier that exposes you, start conversations with them to solve the problem. Look downstream and set the stage for market preference for a product that may be different or cost more but decreases your exposure.

Forced and compulsory labor

Forced labor is defined by the ILO as working under menace of an involuntary penalty. About 21 million people are working in slavery or forced labor.[59] In 2008, a brick-making company in China was exposed for using compulsory labor. Awareness of the business's use of slavery was brought about through the victims' use of the internet to communicate their plight. A Chinese television reporter covered the story, which hit the front cover of the New York Times and BBC News. Eventually, the managers were brought to trial and officials fined or fired.[60]

The Fair Labor label means the supplier has been given a fair price. It is used for agricultural goods from coffee to cotton. In 2011, worldwide fair trade certified sales were 6.6 billion dollars, with 1.2 million farmers in 66 countries.[61]

Theo Chocolates is a small chocolatier located in Seattle that offers premium chocolate and distinguishes itself on its fair labor sourcing. It also distinguishes itself through astute public relations, which includes daily tours of its facility and educational programs. The founders designed the company to be vertically integrated, and spent over a year before entering the market building a manufacturing facility. The company went into production in 2006, and within three years earned revenues of one quarter million dollars.

Forced and compulsory labor

Your youth was rough and tumble, with a period as a member of a biker club and a few stints in the clinker. You came out of it okay though, and today run a clothing business that caters to urban tastes. Your line has gotten popular, and you sell to many of the 'Big Box' stores, including Macy's, Nordstrom, and Kohls. You have a reputation for edgy yet approachable street clothing. Your business model is based on incorporating unknown artists' work. Some of them have gone on to successful careers. Your first line was inspired by tattoo artists. Last year, you used designs inspired by a small gang of graffiti artists from a small town in Texas, and featured the group in your advertisements and labels. The group is in demand by galleries in New York and Europe, which pleases you. Your clothing is designed at your company headquarters in Los Angeles, and you use a long-time business associate to manage the manufacturing. You have never forgotten the Kathy Lee Gifford situation, and the damage to her personal reputation and business for use of child labor in terrible working conditions. Although you have had several conversations with the company that handles your manufacturing, you can't comfortably tell yourself that child labor or unfair labor conditions are not in practice at the facilities that make your clothing. Last week, you read an article in the New York Times about a clothing manufacturing facility in Chittagong, Bangladesh that employs children. The article explained that street children see the manufacturing facility as a refuge from much worse and more dangerous work. The article was not favorable towards the manufacturer. Most of your clothing is manufactured in Chittagong. You are determined to take action to protect your business and address this issue. What's your plan?

What to think about:

- Where to go when between a rock and hard place: if your business is small or medium-sized, you may have no leverage to change your suppliers' working conditions. It may be time to revisit your choice of supplier, and the factors in that decision. If the country of your suppliers is not enforcing labor laws, you may need to look for a supplier in a country where you can rely upon the government to ensure there is fair labor.

- What gives value to your business? In the example, the edginess and the artists' work differentiate the business and are valued by customers. Is there a way to provide this value on an item that enhances the environment and society, such as reusing items, or offering it as a service?

Security practices

One way for a business to ensure the security of its workforce is to hire a security force, or use a nation's armed forces. The United Nations Human

Rights Principles and Responsibilities for Transnational Corporations and Other Business Enterprises includes 18 principles, one of which is for security forces to observe human rights. In Myanmar (Burma), the national armed forces acted as Unocal's security force for its pipeline project. A lawsuit was filed in 1996 under the Alien Tort Claims Act holding Unocal liable for rapes, murder, and acts of forced labor. In 2004, Unocal settled the claim.

Acorn International is a small service provider that helps multinational oil and gas companies assess environmental and social impacts for projects in foreign countries. The company differentiates itself by including information about indigenous peoples and other human rights issues in its work. Acorn's marketing includes annual surveys of the importance players in the oil and gas industry place on human rights, climate change, biodiversity, water resources, and community engagement. It also continually educates clients on the social, environmental, and economic issues of foreign projects. Acorn's clients include Chevron, BP, and Anadarco.

Security practices

You have been a serial entrepreneur your entire life. A few of your businesses shot the moon, and a few have tanked. Last month, you were awarded a low interest loan from your state's Office of Employment, Trade and Economic Development (OETED) to start up small onsite biofuel plants and fuel stations that use agricultural by-products from your state. The supply will be augmented by bamboo from Ecuador and Columbia. You are sourcing through government agencies in these countries. Three private investors are putting in

$1 million each to match the loan. There is a companion grant to a nonprofit that will be offering conversion to biofuel services, educational workshops, and training. Things are looking good, but there is a snag. You know that for the first few years of operations, you will need to import a significant quantity of bamboo until you have the supply lines in place from more local suppliers. You are concerned that indigenous peoples and forests may be displaced to provide bamboo to your business. A large non-profit activist organization has already contacted you and the OETED to ask questions, spurring the OETED to call you. You put them both off for now, but know you will need to reply soon. You do not have a budget in your business plan for ensuring compliance with human rights agreements or habitat protection. What's your plan?

What to think about:

- Understand what is the stage of development of an industry and prepare for the next stage. In the example, some damage to the environment may be necessary to further the development of the clean fuel industry and a strategy is needed for ensuring the industry does not create a different but similar problem in the long run and to restore damage once a business reaches a certain level. This strategy can be communicated to the media, provided to activists as a proposal to work towards, and the basis for business development when partnering with agencies.

Indigenous rights

Indigenous people are often defined as the population that lived on the land before it was colonized or before political boundaries were established.[62] Indigenous peoples have their own culture, language, and traditions. Indigenous traditions are lost when populations are wiped out, communities disintegrate, or peoples are assimilated into a dominant culture. In Hawaii, people of Polynesian, Tahitian, and Menehune descent are considered indigenous. Food plays a large role in the Hawaiian culture. In the 1700s, the island's land fed about half a million indigenous people. By the early 1900s, wars and diseases had brought the population of native Hawaiians down to about 30,000. Of the 1.2 million people living on Hawaii in the early 2000s, approximately 400,000 are descendants of indigenous peoples, and one quarter are fully native.

In 1991, 12 Hawaiian chefs came together to start a movement to foster local food production and preserve the indigenous culture through the food service industry. The Hawaiian Regional Cuisine Movement has helped to create a market for local farmers growing culturally relevant foods. It has also helped chefs including Roy Yamaguchi in his business aspirations. Roy began with one restaurant offering locally sourced foods and a cuisine based on indigenous Hawaiian cooking in 1988. He has expanded off the islands to operate over 30 restaurants throughout the US.

Indigenous rights

You are a career finance officer. You have been working for the same bank for your entire career and today were given a new assignment. Your bank, headquartered in New York and Zurich, acquired a chain of banks in Nova Scotia. You have been asked to spend the next six months transitioning the newly acquired locations. Last week you returned from a vacation in a small town 150 kilometers from Halifax. There you came to understand the plight of the native peoples, who call themselves Mi'kmaq. With only a little over 4000 Mi'kmaq left, many of them are losing their old ways when they go to work for the lumber mills, mining companies, and other businesses. In the last 10 years, there has been an uprising of small businesses, and you suspect that many of the bank's customers are small businesses. You also realize that Canadian laws are more stringent than those in the USA in requiring banks to report on their social performance. You want to set an example with these newly acquired banks for your US and EU colleagues. What's your plan?

What to think about:
- The role of large and medium-sized businesses in fostering small businesses and local communities: a traditional approach to business is to view other companies as competitors. However, most business – up to 80% – is conducted between businesses or 'B2B'. How can your business foster smaller businesses that will become your customers or increase your customer base?

- In North America, every area has an indigenous people and culture associated with it. Many of these cultures are disappearing from the public eye. If handled respectfully, and with consultation and approval by local nations, a business can help customers appreciate indigenous cultures by placing native art and using educational materials in its marketing, brick and mortar locations and otherwise integrating indigenous culture.

CHAPTER 7

Labor Practices and Decent Work: Challenges, Examples, and Opportunities

IN THIS CHAPTER, WE COVER FIVE ASPECTS of labor practices and decent work within the GRI: employment, labor and management relations, occupational health and safety, training and education, and diversity and equal opportunities.

Employment

In the Great Depression of the 1930s, 80% of the value of the stock market disappeared, and upwards of 13 million jobs were lost.[63] Suicide rates escalated, along with homelessness and mental illness. Joblessness caused many tragedies.[64] In 1933, the government responded with a public works program that, among other things, created jobs. It was called the New Deal.

The Hey Group got its start in 1943 in Philadelphia as consultants in organizational development. In 1949, the company expanded into psychological assessments. It helps companies with issues ranging from turnover to compensation and productivity. The company has a strong research arm that guides it in its growth. Helping companies and individuals proved to be profitable for The Hey Group. The company is an international service provider with over 2500 staff and is one of the top 15 highest by revenue in its industry.

Employment

You are the CEO for a placement agency catering to the administration, scientific, and health service industries across the nation and internationally. An important metric your clients use is turnover rate. Over the last five years, you have been receiving more and more resumes requesting work in the sustainability field. While you are able to place many people in the European Union, many qualified applicants are left on file in the USA. Those applicants whom you have placed in the USA have an average tenure of less than two years on the job, much lower than average for people whom you place. You believe this field will grow, but do not want to bring down your average time for a placement. What's your plan?

What to think about:

- Tracking turnover alongside profits: often companies track turnover independent of any financial metric. Within a few years, a company can get an idea of the cost of turnover and thus better understand the benefits of allocating funds and resources towards employee retention.

- Workforce development in a new field or industry

> can be costly for a company. In this example, new employees demand for sustainability jobs outstripped the company's ability to supply jobs. Internships can be a low cost way to develop a workforce, gain some benefit to the company, and foster growth of a new field.

Labor–management relations

On 25 March 1911, 146 workers were killed in a fire at Triangle Shirtwaist Company in New York. Two years earlier, walk-outs by Triangle Shirtwaist Company workers spurred a strike by over 20,000 garment workers. Employees were protesting the dangerous working conditions. Flammable materials were loosely stored beside open gaslights. Workers were allowed to smoke on the floor. The average workweek was between 60 and 72 hours and wages were well below the average paid in the day. It was not uncommon to see 12 or 13-year-olds at sewing machines. Rather than listen to their staff, the owners of the company struck back by hiring thugs to intimidate the protesting employees.

A fire broke out on the eighth floor. No one told the employees on the ninth floor until it was too late. Even then, one of the two doors out was locked. The fire escape was defunct. Sixty-two women jumped to their death. Eighty-four died in the fire. The next day, 80,000 people gathered in the streets of Manhattan to mourn and protest. Twenty-seven years later, in 1938, Congress passed the Fair Labor Standards Act (FLSA) requiring a minimum wage, maximum hours worked, and prohibiting child labor.[65]

The first 100 years of the Minnesota Mining and Manufacturing Company (3M) began in 1902, producing, mining, and manufacturing grinding wheels and sandpaper. At the onset, the company had problems with quality, and things did not look good for the investors. Management found a solution by asking employees to come up with creative solutions. 3M's approach to labor-management relations has been based on programs and a culture allowing employees to express and develop their creativity.[66] The relationship between management and workers is sometimes called '3M Way'.[67] Practices of the 3M Way include the 15 Percent Rule or Structured Serendipity, and the Benevolent Blind Eye. Under the 15 Percent Rule, workers can spend up to 15% of their time on innovation. Innovation is defined at 3M as a creative idea that is implemented and ultimately viable in the marketplace.[68] Workers can also approach management to gain access to resources for their projects. Structured Serendipity calls upon management to encourage workers to explore ideas and new products while working on a project. Under the Benevolent Blind Eye principle, managers and workers come to an understanding that a certain amount of risk is encouraged and failure tolerated. Workers are also permitted to take the time they need to test products, whether that be a few months or years.

Labor-management relations

You run an architecture and urban design firm with offices in six major cities on the east coast. You keep your edge in the industry by engaging in one cutting-edge project a year. You know you will not make money on this project, but it may help you strengthen a market or break into a new market. Staff volunteer their time on these projects. Your marketing team loves these projects, and features them on your website and at conferences. Last year, your project was a design for an off-the-grid mixed-use conservation community on the Mississippi Gulf Coast engineered to withstand hurricane force winds, restore wetlands, and establish fisheries. In the last few years, you have had a drastic increase in staff who are willing to volunteer their time for the projects. Last year, you had to deny 70 staff for the project. You are also hearing a pretty consistent complaint from your managers about the work ethic of today's youth. They tell you that new hires emphasize work–life balance and want an average of seven weeks a year off. Many are willing to take time off without pay. You are concerned the future profitability of the firm. What's your plan?

What to think about:

- Inspiring employees coupled with motivation by sustainability can result in high yields to your company. Programs for inspiration can come in many forms: volunteer opportunities to work on cutting-edge sustainability related projects where employees have the feeling they are contributing to solving a large problem or encouragement to identify problems and solutions in the business process that increase the company's sustainability performance.

- Work–life balance is increasingly a big issue for

employees. Policies allowing part-time work are growing common. Reorienting your company towards part-time workers rather than favoring full-time positions could help increase retention and boost productivity while solving the work–life balance issue. As with measuring retention, tracking profits alongside part-time and full-time employees will demonstrate whether part-time employees are good for a company or not.

Occupational health and safety

Asbestos manufacturing workers, or their families, tell stories of returning home from work looking like snowmen. These are often fond memories tainted by despair from dealing with mesothelioma, asbestosis, and other diseases caused by exposure to asbestos.

The Greeks and Romans wove asbestos into fabric and used it for its fire resistant qualities over 2000 years ago. With the industrial age, the asbestos industry caught hold. Hundreds of asbestos products hit the marketplace, ranging from bricks to break pads, oven parts and stage curtains. Manufacturing asbestos became big business. Asbestosis was named as a disease in 1924. In spite of mounting scientific evidence that asbestos was putting the lives of workers and their families at risk, some companies refused to make changes, not even to take safety precautions or tell workers of the risks. Approximately 27 million workers in America were exposed to asbestos on the job.

By 2001, approximately $58 billion had been spent on legal costs and compensation for asbestos-related claims and over 65 companies had filed for bankruptcy from the claims.[69] Some estimates tally the costs of claims by workers and others affected by exposure to asbestos at over 250 billion dollars.[70] This does not include any potential suits by claimants in developing nations, where asbestos is still being manufactured into building, automotive, and other parts.

Alcoa set a goal for zero work-related injuries and illness in 1987. At that time, annual revenues were $1.5 billion. They wanted to test the theory that healthy workers and a safe work environment open the door to greater profits.[71] They tracked fatalities, lost workdays due to injuries, the injury rate, and rate of facilities offering training in culture and health issues. Twenty years after the safety goal was set, Alcoa hit revenues of $30 billion and a net income of $2.98 billion, roughly double 1987's annual revenues. No doubt many other factors contributed to Alcoa's success, including profit-sharing programs, leveling of the hierarchical managerial structure, increases in the research and development budget, an emphasis on recycling, and installing the latest technology at the plants. However, safety first continues to be a focus of the firm, with the understanding that a healthy workforce and safe workplace drives up profits and allows the company to meet revenue goals.

Occupational health and safety

Your company has been providing popular microwaveable snacks since the 1970s when microwaves became popular and affordable. You have plants in the United States, Mexico, and Canada. All your products are approved for consumption by the US Food and Drug Administration, Canadian Food Inspection Agency, and the Federal Commission for Protection against Health Risks in Mexico. Last year, you received a report from one of your plants showing a substantial increase in sick days and one worker's death after a stay at a hospital. This year, sick days are increasing in several other plants. Your main competitors have been named in lawsuits by their employees and the families of three deceased employees. You are concerned about the future of your company, and want to take action to demonstrate that you care about your employees. What's your plan?

What to think about:

- A great deal of information can be found in the trenches. Managers who regularly go onto the work floor or spend time in the office with all level of employees can get a better picture of employee realities. With relationships comes trust and employees can open up to managers and tell them of concerns. Because employees have direct experience with their working conditions, as opposed to scientists who study impacts and issue reports to inform regulators on health and safety, a manager can garner important information about the health and safety of the company from employees.

> - Look at the problems your competitors are facing as low-cost opportunities for you to learn and improve. If your competitor is being sued, and the issue is material, it will show up in their financial statements. This is another place for low-cost learning.

Training and education

One hundred years ago, on-the-job training or professional development was an anomaly. If an employee was trained, the training occurred at the beginning of his or her career, and then did his or her job for the course of employment. The need for people to learn through their lives was not widely contemplated by employers. Nor were the implications of the dearth of training until this century. It was only in the roaring '20s that doctors were required to maintain their knowledge, and much later for lawyers.[72,73]

In 2002, Turner, a construction company, opened Turner University for their employees and business partners. They aimed to 'enhance job performance and personal goals' for staff and 'strengthen relationships with partners'.[74] A year later it opened the university to the general public. In 2004, Turner announced their commitment to green building.[75] By 2008, they partnered with the US Green Building Council to offer online courses for staff, partners, and the public to train for LEED accreditation tests. By then, they were one of the largest green construction companies in the United States, with $3 billion of its $10.6 billion annual revenues coming from green building.

Training and education

You have been running a Health Management Organization (HMO) that caters to rural communities in the Midwest for 12 years. Five years ago you started outsourcing diagnosis of standard procedure tests to India. From the outset, you received superior service at a fraction of the costs. Today, your hospitals send millions of dollars of work to India. The HMO is doing well, and many of your hospitals are expanding operations. Your human resources department came to you last week with a request for guidance. They have not been able to find enough doctors with US nationality to fill the positions at the hospitals and so are hiring doctors from South East Asia, India, and Africa. In some of the communities, these doctors are not being well received. The hospital is getting complaints from the doctors and members of communities. You believe this issue also needs to be raised with the board. How will you frame the issue to the board, and what alternatives will you suggest to them?

What to think about:

- Think risk management for training programs: training programs are often focused on further developing skills directly related to job performance. However, greater returns can come from designing training programs to avoid risk. In the example, doctors are at increased risk of being sued when they do not have good relationships with patients, and doctors who are liked and trusted by their patients are least likely to be sued. Yet most of their professional training does not address relationship building or interpersonal skills. Similarly, in many businesses, lawsuits and costly mistakes come from interpersonal issues and poor communication which can be addressed through training programs to develop people-skills.

Diversity and equal opportunity

Diversity is often defined in terms of gender, race, ethnicity, physical ability, sexual orientation, and age. Other diversity factors include class, place of birth or home, parental status, marital status, political or religious affiliations, and work experience. Equal opportunity is a way to describe fairness in hiring and treatment of workers. Within Fortune 500 companies, women held 7.6% of the top earning positions in 2010.[76] In 1996, only one woman held the CEO position of a Fortune 500 company.[77] In 2014, there are only 41 women CEOs among the Fortune 1000 companies. As of 2004, 7.2% of the Fortune 1000 in the United States had more than two women as top managers.[78] In 2011, women held slightly over 15% of all board positions in Fortune 500 companies.[79] Fifty of the Fortune 500 companies have exclusively male boards of directors, and for 393 Fortune 500 company boards, women are 25% or less of the board.[79]

In 2002, Pepsico launched its Women of Color Multicultural Alliance. The aim of the program was to increase the diversity of the staff through hiring and retention. 'Power Pairs' were formed whereby managers mentored staff members. In 2008, 10% of managers and 7% of senior managers were multicultural women. Four of the 10 members of its board of directors are women. In 2006 Pepsico appointed its first women CEO, Indra Nooyi. Her mandate, called 'performance with purpose', is to gain half the company's revenue from healthful products. In the words of Pepsico's CEO, performance with purpose 'doesn't mean subtracting from the bottom line. . . but. . . that we bring together what is good for business with what is good for the world'.[80] Annual revenues jumped to $25 billion in 2002, $35 billion in 2006, and $43 billion dollars in 2008.

Diversity and equal opportunity

Your construction company found its niche in engineering and constructing low-income housing for governments in the early 1960s. Affirmative action laws were key in getting your first projects. Today, your company is an easy fit for the emerging market in providing housing for first homebuyers in the medium-income bracket. All the signs point to your company winning a large project for mixed subsidized housing and medium-income first-time homeowners. Environmental justice is a high priority for the decision-makers who will award the project. They define environmental justice as equity among all segments of the population in bearing the burdens of environmental hazards and meaningful involvement of all stakeholders in decisions. The project will be closely watched, as it is one of the first on its scale. The site is adjacent to industrial sites that are closed now due to contamination. Your plans include provisions to protect inhabitants from contamination on the site. However, a public meeting revealed the communities' concerns about health impacts from adjacent site contaminants. You need to find a way to demonstrate environmental justice while staying competitive on the bid. What's your plan?

What to think about:

- Social justice cannot be addressed or reached without involvement in decisions of the parties historically oppressed and currently impacted by the issue at hand. Hiring practices that ensure women, minorities, or others in the workforce and management reflect the population is one way to ensure involvement. In the example, involving the community in discovery of the issues they cared about and in finding solutions is another way. This is costly, takes time, and can be complicated. However, for a complicated project, it is often less costly to involve the community early on than in response to a problem down the road.

CHAPTER 8

Conclusion:
You Get What You Measure

THIS BOOK PRESENTS YOU WITH A LANDSCAPE of sustainability reporting. It gives you ideas for how business practices can provide profitable solutions to sustainability challenges. More importantly, it gives you an idea of what you can measure in your business. And this is a key step for sustainability reporting.

You can't manage what you can't measure. The Global Reporting Initiative began with the vision that if business managers like you measured the areas of sustainability, disasters could be averted and businesses could find solutions to the biggest challenges facing us in the future: our own sustainability.

Now that you understand what sustainability is for a business, the next step is to identify what you will manage and how you will measure that business performance. One way to do this is to indentify what you are already managing and measuring in the areas of sustainability. To do this, you need to assess your business performance as it stands today. You will probably find that you are already managing some areas and aspects of sustainability, but were not calling it that. With this in mind, we conclude this book with a series of simple charts you can use to assess your business's status in the sustainability landscape. Use the charts to get an idea of your own knowledge and knowledge gaps for your company.

For each chart, you will find a list of performance areas you are probably already measuring and managing as well as pointers on where to find the data and next steps for that area. (Please note, the bulleted lists below are not complete. They are a distillation of indicators in the Global Reporting Initiative, and cover only performance areas that your company is most likely to be measuring or that are relatively easy for you to start measuring.)

TABLE 1. Economic aspects checklist

Economic aspects	Are you measuring this aspect?
Economic performance	
Market presence	
Indirect economic impacts	

Below is a list of economic activity you probably already manage and data you can include in your sustainability report. Most of the information you can gather from your accounting, marketing and human resources departments. The challenge will likely be that many people within your company are managing the various performance areas, and so gathering the information from them will take some patience and time.

- Organizational profile – name, description of services or goods, organizational structure (divisions, subsidiaries, joint ventures)

- Financial performance – income statement, balance sheet, businesses strategy, government assists and payments

- Places of operation and points of sale – include a map of your suppliers, offices or factories, and places of sale

- Local minimum wages compared to standard entry level wages for each place of business

- Local suppliers and hires – proportion of local supply, local hiring

- Investments in local communities – infrastructure development, services provided

One easy step for your first sustainability report is including environmental, social, and other performance reporting in your annual report, rather than issuing a separate sustainability report. This sends a message to investors, customers, and the public that your company takes its sustainability performance seriously. It also sends a message to your employees that you are integrating sustainability measures and performance into day-to-day activities of the company. You do not need to report on every aspect of sustainability in your first report. Instead, you can include only those you already have data for, and explain your strategy in the company overview section.

TABLE 2. Environment and aspects checklist

Environment aspects	Are you measuring this aspect?
Materials	
Energy	
Water	
Biodiversity	
Emissions, effluents, & waste	

Products and services

Compliance

Transport

Overall – environmental protection
expenditures and investments

Below is a list of environmental activity you probably already manage and what you can include in your sustainability report. You can probably gather a lot of this information from your accounting department and plant or office manager. One of the challenges in gathering this data and later managing environmental performance will be reconciling dates and time. For example, data about energy use may be on a monthly cycle, while for materials on a quarterly cycle.

- Materials used – type and amount used, amount recycled

- Energy – type and amount of energy consumed, conserved, and energy efficiency or reduction programs

- Water used – amount used and source, amount recycled and reused

- Greenhouse gas and other emissions, activities to reduce emissions

- Waste by type and amount

- Activities to reduce environmental impact in operations and from products or services

The first step many companies take towards measuring and managing sustainability is a greenhouse gas emissions inventory. Most companies will measure only what they have control over. For a service business, greenhouse gas emissions will be drawn from energy bills, air and auto travel records and, to some extent, suppliers and waste. This measurement is often paired with the formation or furthering of 'green teams' which come up with ideas for reducing emissions in the work place, in marketing, and in your goods and services. Green teams are often self-selected employees from every level of a company who meet on a regular basis. Their activities can be rich sources for your sustainability management and reporting in the environmental and other areas of performance.

You may not want some of the data in this area or others included in a sustainability report for the public, such as notices of violations or lawsuits. In addition, gathering this information may cause your employees consternation, some of it warranted. To this, it is important to make it clear that the purpose of your first data gathering is for internal use only, and that you will report publicly only select data.

TABLE 3. Society and aspects checklist

Society aspects	Are you measuring this aspect?
Community	
Corruption	
Public policy	
Anti-competitive behavior	
Compliance	

CONCLUSION:
YOU GET WHAT YOU MEASURE

Below is a list of activity in the society area you probably already manage and that you can include in your sustainability report. You will probably find information for this section from your marketing department for activities in the community and the legal department for the rest. For a manufacturing company, you may want to also ask facilities managers for notice of non-compliance in addition to the legal department. One of the challenges with gathering data for the society aspect is the qualitative nature of the data. Another is the sensitive nature of the information.

- Charitable activities, donations, and programs

- Anti-corruption policies and programs

- Public policy positions, lobbying activities, and political contributions

- Notices or fines for non-compliance with any laws or regulations

- Lawsuits by the company or against the company

Reporting on your company and employee's charitable activities is a low hanging fruit in sustainability management and reporting. A benefit of this exercise is the information can help you to leverage your position in society. Often in companies, the marketing, public relations, or legal department already gathers and reports this data, and the person in that department who has been managing this data has a strategy and is eager to share his or her ideas with company decision-makers.

On the other hand, the data about lawsuits, non-compliance, public policy positions, and anti-corruption policies often brings up difficult and complex management issues. For these areas of performance, a survey of company policies, measures for those policies, and goal setting can be a powerful step. That said, this is often a longer-term project and this data is not included in most companies first public sustainability report.

TABLE 4. Product responsibility aspects checklist

Product responsibility aspects	Are you measuring this aspect?
Customer health & safety	
Product & service labeling	
Marketing communications	
Customer privacy	
Compliance	

Below is a list of product responsibility activities you probably already manage and what you can include in your sustainability reporting. Your marketing department will likely be the repository for most of the data in the product responsibility area. For manufacturing companies, the operations department may have data as well.

- Customer health and safety policies or codes and programs

- Customer satisfaction activities – surveys and survey results

- Marketing standards and programs

- Customer privacy policy and programs

- Incidence of non-compliance with laws protecting the consumers

One easy first step to reporting your product responsibility performance is reporting data about customer satisfaction. Your company's policies for customer health and safety are another low hanging fruit for your first sustainability report. Determining measures and goals to manage those policies are a next step, and may take some time.

When there is no data for the other aspects of product responsibility performance, you can start measuring and managing performance by setting policies and working with managers to determine how to measure their performance to those policies. The next step after that is often goal setting.

TABLE 5. Labor practices and decent work aspects checklist

Labor practices and decent work aspects	Are you measuring this aspect?
Employment	
Labor–management relations	
Occupational health & safety	
Training & education	
Diversity & equal opportunity	

Below is a list of labor practices and decent work activities you probably already manage and what you can include in your sustainability reporting. You can likely look to your human resources department for labor practices data.

- Employees – by region and type, employee turnover

- Diversity report – employees, management and governance by gender and minority

- Employee development – average hours of training, skill development, and learning programs

- Employee performance review – percent of employees receiving review

Many human resources departments do not collect a lot of data in the labor practices and decent work area. In addition, collecting this data may be met with resistance. If this is the case, setting policies can be a good first step. One policy may focus on increasing the diversity in the workforce, management, or governance. Another may be to ensure annual performance reviews for all staff. A third can be focused on programs for staff development or skill training, such as mentoring.

TABLE 6. Human rights aspects checklist

Human rights aspects	Are you measuring this aspect?
Investment & procurement practices	
Non-discrimination	
Freedom of association & collective bargaining	
Child labor	
Forced & compulsory labor	
Security practices	
Indigenous rights	

Below is a list of human rights activities you probably already manage and what you can include in your sustainability reporting. Your legal or human resources department will likely have the information you need for this section. This area is more relevant to companies providing goods with manufacturing facilities or suppliers in developing nations. For small and medium-sized companies operating entirely in one country, many of the aspects of human rights will not be relevant.

- Anti-discrimination policy and programs

- Human rights, forced labor, and child labor– policies, programs, and measures

Your company may not be collecting any data on aspects of human rights, and you may not have any policies. If this is the case, putting in place an anti-discrimination policy is a good first step. It will not make sense to have polices, programs, measures, or goals for human rights or against forced or child labor if your company does not face these issues or do business in countries where these issues are present. In this case, simply stating this is enough for your report.

Your company's sustainability assessment

Once you have an idea of the areas and aspects of sustainability that your company is managing and measuring, you are ready to conduct a full assessment. This entails gathering information from your staff. For your assessment you can use a chart for internal data gathering so you can track the data to its source, manage performance, and form a plan for future data gathering. A chart with the fields for your assessment is below.

TABLE 7. Sustainability assessment chart

Area and aspect of performance	
Measure	
Department	
Manager	
Source	
Goal set?	
Timing of data reporting	
Notes	

Your assessment provides the information for your first sustainability report. It is also a launching pad for your sustainability strategy. Your company will more successfully increase profits by integrating sustainability into its business performance seamlessly. I explain how to do this in my next book in this series *Sustainability Decoded*.

References

1. Facts from the World Resource Institute (WRI) and the United Nation's Environment Programme's Millennium Assessment.

2. Lobovikov, M. et al. 2007. World bamboo resources: A thematic study prepared in the framework of the Global Forest Resources Assessment 2005. *Non-Wood Forest Products* (Volume 18): 1–88.

3. US Energy Information Administration, Official Energy Statistics from the US Government, available at: **http://tonto.eia.doe.gov/cfapps/ipdbproject/IED Index3.cfm?tid=5&pid=54&aid=2.**

4. Development, Security, and Cooperation (DSC). 2007. *Energy Futures and Urban Air Pollution: Challenges for China and the United States* (Washington, DC: The National Academies).

5. Energy Information Administration, Official Energy Statistic from the US Government, available at: **http://www.eia.doe.gov/pub/oil_gas/petroleum/ analysis_publications/oil_market_basics/demand_text.htm#GlobalOil Consumption.**

6. Hawken, P. et al. 1999. *Natural Capitalism* (New York: Hachett Book Group).

7. Solomon S. et al. 2007. Contribution of Working Group I to the Fourth Assessment Report of the Intergovernmental Panel on Climate Change. *Intergovernmental Panel on Climate Change* (Technical Summary) TS.3.

8. Granade, H. et al. 2007. *California Climate Change Portal & Greenhouse Gas Emissions Report* (McKinsey & Company).

9. World Resource Institute. 2008. *World Green House Gas Emissions Flow Chart* (Washington, DC: World Resource Institute).

10. US EPA. 2008. Municipal solid waste in the United States. Facts and Fixtures EPA (530-R-08-010), available at: www.epa.gov/epawaste/nonhaz/municipal/pubs/msw08-rpt.pdf.

11. Marks, L. and Howden, D. 2008. The world's rubbish dump: A garbage tip that stretches from Hawaii to Japan. *The Independent*, 5 February, available at: http://www.independent.co.uk/environment/green-living/the-worlds-rubbish-dump-a-tip-that-stretches-from-hawaii-to-japan-778016.html.

12. fundinguniverse.com. 2009. Available at: http://www.greenbiz.com/news/2009/03/09/patagonias-clothing-recycling-program-lessons-learned-challenges-ahead.

13. United Nations. 2008. *Vital Water Graphics, An Overview of the State of the World's Fresh and Marine Waters*, 2nd edn (New York: UN).

14. Mueller, J. 2008. How much water do you really use? The truth may shock you. *CSR News Wire*, 8 January.

15. *Infochange* (Corporate Responsibility). 2004. Manipadma Jena Steel City tackles its water woes, available at: http://infochangeindia.org/corporate-responsibility/features/steel-city-tackles-its-water-woes.html.

16. IUCN. 2008. Redlist, available at: http://www.iucnredlist.org/about/summary-statistics.

17. Kricher, J. 2008. *The Ecological Planet: An Introduction to Earth's Major Ecosystems* (Wheaton, IL: Wheaton College Press).

18. McKay, K. et al. 2006. *True Green: 100 Everyday Ways You Can Contribute to a Healthier Planet* (Des Moines, IA: National Geographic Books).

19. *Environmental Leader*. 2006. Wal-Mart packaging reduction plan could save $11 billion, available at: http://www.environmentalleader.com/2006/09/25/wal-mart-packaging-reduction-plan-could-save-11-billion/.

20. US EPA. 2009. *Annual Non-Compliance Report, NPDES System Non-Majors* (Washington, DC: US EPA).

21. US EPA. 2007. *Annual Non-Compliance Report (ANCR) on NPDES Non-Majors* (Washington, DC: US EPA).

22. US Natural Resources Defense Council. 1998. *America's Animal Factories: How States Fail to Prevent Pollution from Livestock Waste* (New York: Natural Resources Defense Council).

23. Fresh Breeze Organics, available at: http://www.freshbreezeorganic.com/contact/html.

24. HUD.GOV. Brownfields frequently asked questions, available at: http://www.hud.gov/offices/cpd/economicdevelopment/programs/bedi/bfieldsfaq.cfm.

25. US Census Bureau. 2008. Employers and nonemployer data, available at: http://www.census.gov/econ/smallbus.html.

26. US Department of Commerce. 2011. Economics & statistics administration, business startups: Why entrepreneurs didn't start up in 2009 and why that's likely to change, available at: http://www.esa.doc.gov/Blog/2011/03/23/business-startups-why-entrepreneurs-didnt-start-2009-and-why-thats-likely-change.

27. Ibid.

28. US Small Business Administration. FAQ, available at: http://web.sba.gov/faqs/faqindex.cfm?areaID=24.

29. Goldfarb, B. et al. 2006. Will dotcom bubble burst again? *Los Angeles Times Discussion*, available at: http://qctimes.com/business/will-dotcom-bubble-burst-again/article_114ea0f5-677a-5487-8f16-de1faca2dddd.html.

30. US Bureau of Labor & Statistics. 2009. After the dot-com bubble: Silicon Valley high-tech employment and wages in 2001 and 2008, available at: http://www.bls.gov/opub/regional_reports/200908_silicon_valley_high_tech.htm.

31. Goldfarb, B. et al. 2006. Was there too little entry during the dot com era? Robert H. Smith School Research Paper (No. RHS 06-029), available at: http://ssrn.com/abstract=899100.

32. Hamm, S. and Lashaman, N. 2007. The trouble with India: Crumbling roads, jammed airports, and power blackouts could hobble growth. *Business Week Online*, 19 March.

33. *USA Today*. 2007. Chaos at New Delhi airport highlights India's infrastructure woes, available at: http://usatoday30.usatoday.com/travel/flights/2007-01-04-delhi-airport_x.htm.

34. Runckel, C. 2007. Infrastructure India: A long road ahead. **Business-in-Asia.com**, available at: http://www.business-in-asia.com/asia/infrastructure_india.html.

35. National Coalition for the Homeless. 2009. How many people experience homelessness?, available at: http://www.nationalhomeless.org/factsheets/How_Many.html.

36. Transparency International. 2011. The Corruption Perception Index 2011, available at: http://cpi.transparency.org/cpi2011/.

37. *The Fiscal Times*. 2011. The ten largest global business corruption cases, 13 December, available at: http://www.thefiscaltimes.com/Articles/2011/12/13/The-Ten-Largest-Global-Business-Corruption-Cases.aspx#page1.

38. *Sawyer*. 2010. Ben and Jerry's Ice Cream start up story, 8 December, available at: http://sawyerspeaks.com/start-up-story-ben-and-jerrys-ice-cream/.

39. *Associated Press*. 2006. Ben & Jerry's back to roots, seeking social change: Ice cream company founders leading new pro-children campaign, 11 July, available at: http://www.msnbc.msn.com/id/13819483/ns/business-us_business/t/ben-jerry-back-roots-seeking-social-change/#.UK52xuOe_5E.

40. Open Secrets. Lobbying database, available at: http://www.opensecrets.org.

41. Richardson, J. 2009. A list of corporate lobbying. *Organic Consumers.org*, 18 June, available at: http://www.organicconsumers.org/articles/article_18394.cfm.

42. Attkisson, S. 2008. Big three spending millions on lobbying. *CBS News Investigate*, 3 December, available at: http://www.cbsnews.com/2100-500690_162-4646424.html.

43. Open Secrets. 2009. TARP recipients paid out $114 million for politicking last year, available at: http://www.opensecrets.org/news/2009/02/tarp-recipients-paid-out-114-m.html.

44. MoneyNews.com. 2009. Bailout firms using money to lobby Congress, 21 July, available at: http://moneynews.newsmax.com/economy/bailout/2009/07/21/238126.html.

45. *State of Illinois*, 2004–2007. Progress reports for Wrigley, available at: http://www.ilcorpacct.com/corpacct/ProgressReport.aspx.

46. United States Department of Justice. 2012. Criminal program update, Spring, available at: http://www.justice.gov/atr/public/division-update/2012/criminal-program.html.

47. Volokh, E. 2003. Nike and the Free-Speech Knot. *Wall Street Journal*, June 30.

48. Fugimoto, M. et al. 2008. Importing products: Legal risks and defense strategies. *Defense Council Journal* (Volume 75, Number 3): 238–243.

49. *Lawyers and Settlements.com*. 2011. Mattel toy recalls, August, available at: http://www.lawyersandsettlements.com/lawsuit/mattel-toys-lead-paint-testing.html#.UFN8baSe5j4.

50. McGinnis, J. et al. 2006. *Food Marketing to Children: Threat or Opportunity?* (Washington, DC: National Academies Press).

51. Wolf, C. and Tobin, C. 2011. *Proskauer on International Litigation and Dispute Resolution: Managing, Resolving, and Avoiding Cross-Border Business or Regulatory Disputes* (Proskauer Rose LLP), available at: http://www.proskauerguide.com/law_topics/28/II.

52. Law, M. 2004. *History of Food and Drug Regulation in the United States*. EH.Net Encyclopedia, available at: http://eh.net/encyclopedia/article/Law.Food.and.Drug.Regulation.

53. Killkenny, Allison. 2012. Occupy plans take down of Bank of America. *The Nation*, 9 April, available at: http://www.thenation.com/blog/167286/occupys-plans-take-down-bank-america#.

REFERENCES

54. Amnesty International USA. 2006. Conflict diamond, available at: http://www. amnestyusa.org/our-work/issues/business-and-human-rights/oil-gas-and-mining-industries/conflict-diamonds.

55. National Partnership for Women and Families. 2004. Women at work: Looking behind the numbers. 40 years after the Civil Rights Act of 1964, available at: http://www.nationalpartnership.org/site/PageServer?pagename=ourwork_wpd; Workplace Discrimination & Goldman Sachs. 1999. Womenomics, 13 August, available at: http://www.goldmansachs.com/our-thinking/topics/women-and-economics/womenomics-2011/index.html; 2008. Women hold up half the sky. *Goldman & Sachs Global Economic Paper* Number 164, March, available at: http://www.goldmansachs.com/our-thinking/topics/women-and-economics/women-hold-up-half-the-sky.html.

56. Katz, N. 2008. Equality in the workplace: Can women break the glass ceiling? *Associated Content, Business & Finance*, 13 August, available at: http://voices. yahoo.com/equality-workplace-women-break-glass-1789485.html.

57. Greenhouse, S. 2011. Union membership in U.S. fell to a 70-year low last year. *The New York Times*, January, available at: http://www.nytimes.com/2011/01/22/business/22union.html?adxnnl=1&adxnnlx=1353617511-+inX4B+L2VGpt M9GZbO9TQ.

58. Fyfe, A. 2007. The worldwide movement against child labor progress and future directions (Geneva: International Labor Office); Chanthavong, S. 2002. *Chocolate and slavery: Child Labor in the Cote d'Ivoire* (American University TED Case Studies Number 664).

59. ILO. 2012. 21 million people are now victims of forced labor, ILO says, available at: http://www.ilo.org/global/about-the-ilo/newsroom/news/WCMS_181961/lang--en/index.htm.

60. *BBC News.* 2007. Chinese slave labour trial begins, 4 July, available at: http://news.bbc.co.uk/2/hi/asia-pacific/6268280.stm.

61. Global Fairtrade Resource Network, 2012. Certified sales grow 12% from 6.6B in 2011, 18 July, available at: http://www.fairtraderesource.org/2012/07/18/global-fairtrade-certified-sales-grow-12-to-6-6b-in-2011/.

62. ILO. 2004. Workshop on data collection and disaggregation for indigenous peoples. ILO Convention No. 169 & The Concept of Indigenous Peoples, Department of Economic and Social Affairs, New York, 19–21.

63. Taylor, T. 2008. A short history of the Great Depression. *New York Times*, available at: http://topics.nytimes.com/top/reference/timestopics/subjects/g/great_depression_1930s/index.html.

64. Ibid.

65. Sociology at Duke University. 1996. Now & then timeline. Soc 142 Organizations & Global Competitiveness, available at: http://www.soc.duke.edu/courses/soc142/time.html.

66. Hindo, B. 2007. At 3M, a struggle between efficiency and creativity. Inside innovation in depth. *Business Week*, 30 June, available at: http://www.businessweek.com/magazine/content/07_24/b4038406.htm.

67. Grundling, E. 2000. *The 3M Way to Innovation: Balancing People and Profit* (Tokyo: Kodansha International).

68. Ibid.

69. Carroll, S. et al. 2002. Asbestos litigation costs and compensation. Rand Interim Report, available at: http://www.rand.org/pubs/documented_briefings/DB397.html.

70. Woellert, L. 2003. Will a chance for asbestos reform be missed? *Business Week Online*, 13 January, available at: www.businessweek.com:/print/magazine/content/03_.02/b3815036.htm); Carroll, S. et al. 2002. Asbestos litigation costs and compensation. Rand Interim Report, available at: http://www.rand.org/pubs/documented_briefings/DB397.html.

71. Oxenburgh, M. et al., 2004. *Increasing Productivity & Profit through Health and Safety* (London: Taylor & Francis) and 2004. Health and safety information in small businesses. *Health and Safety Works*, Belfast, available at: http://www.healthandsafetyworksni.gov.uk/an_introduction_to_health_and_safety__version_3__february_2010.pdf.

REFERENCES

72. Josseran, L. and Chaperon, J. 2001. History of continuing medical education in the United States. *Presse Med* (Volume 30: Issue 10): 493–497.

73. Top Green Contractors. 2008. Engineering news record, available at: http://enr.construction.com/toplists/greencontractors/001-100.asp.

74. *Turner Construction News Release*. 2004. Turner Construction Company announces the rollout of Turner Knowledge Network (TKN) and Turner University (TM) Online to the general public, available at: http://www.prnewswire.com/news-releases/turner-construction-company-announces-the-rollout-of-turner-knowledge-network-tkn-and-turner-universitytm-online-to-the-general-public-74550982.html.

75. *Turner Construction News Release*. 2004. Turner announces formal commitment to green building practices, available at: http://www.prnewswire.com/news-releases/turner-construction-announces-formal-commitment-to-green-building-practices-73930012.html.

76. Soares, R. et al. 2011. 2011 Catalyst Census: Fortune 500 women executive officers and top earners. Ernst & Young, December, available at: http://www.catalyst.org/publication/516/2011-catalyst-census-fortune-500-women-executive-officers-and-top-earners.

77. Jones, D. 2009. Women CEOs slowly gain on Corporate America. *USA Today*, January, available at: http://usatoday30.usatoday.com/money/companies/management/2009-01-01-women-ceos-increase_N.htm.

78. Helfat, C. et al. 2006. The pipeline to the top: Women and men executives in U.S. corporations. *Academy of Management Perspectives* (Volume 20: Issue 3) 1–53, available at: http://www.luc.edu/umc/newsroom/publishedstudies/dawnharris.pdf.

79. Soares, R. et al. 2011. 2011 Catalyst Census: Fortune 500 women executive officers and top earners. Ernst & Young, December, available at: http://www.catalyst.org/publication/516/2011-catalyst-census-fortune-500-women-executive-officers-and-top-earners.

80. Useem, M. 2008. America's best leaders: Indra Nooyi, PepsiCo CEO. *US News & World Report*, 19 November, available at: **http://www.usnews.com/news/best-leaders/articles/2008/11/19/americas-best-leaders-indra-nooyi-pepsico-ceo.**

For Product Safety Concerns and Information please contact our EU
representative GPSR@taylorandfrancis.com
Taylor & Francis Verlag GmbH, Kaufingerstraße 24, 80331 München, Germany

www.ingramcontent.com/pod-product-compliance
Ingram Content Group UK Ltd.
Pitfield, Milton Keynes, MK11 3LW, UK
UKHW040928180425
457613UK00011B/307